bio
tope

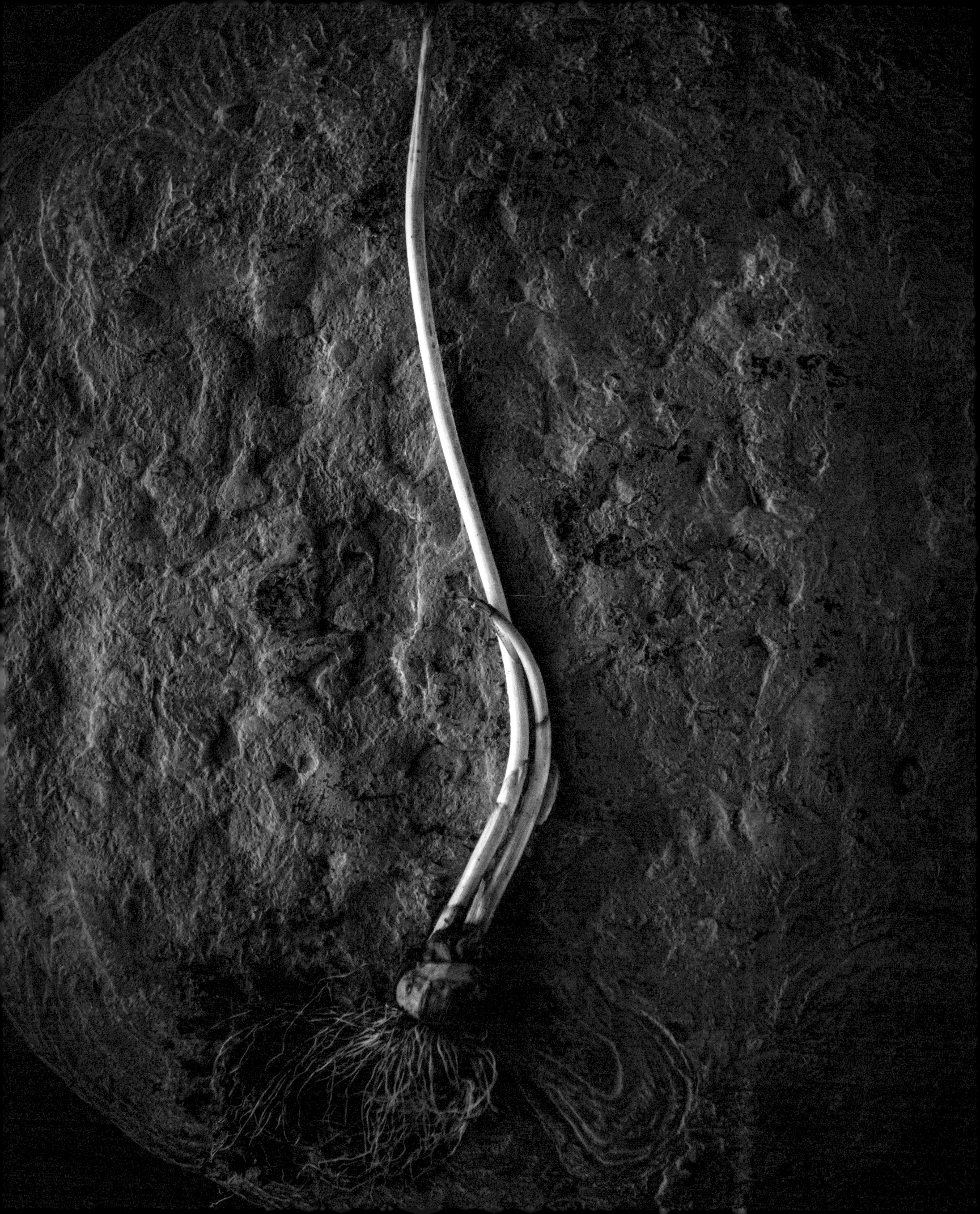

biotope

PASTORALE - BART DE POOTER

TEXT: ROBBY SALLAETS

PHOTOGRAPHY: KRIS VLEGELS

LANNOO

13 MAY 1968
14 MAY 2019

Introduction

There comes a time in your life that calls for reflection, a time to look back on all of your achievements and to look forward to what the future may hold. With this book I would like to introduce you to my world and live my life with me as a chef, businessman and father. I would like to introduce you to those people and experiences that have taken me to a higher level. You will meet the real stars, those who helped me to turn Pastorale into a reality, but you will also be introduced to the people who made me into what I am and the people I have worked with on a variety of projects. I have learned so much from so many people around me that all I can do now is to express my gratitude. With this book I hope to repay this debt, if only in small measures. Not only am I talking about my career highs and lows, I'm also keen to share what I have learned along the way. My favourite kitchen techniques as well as my own stories and recipes that helped to put Pastorale on the menu, plus my passion for art paired with a gastronomic dining experience.

I can only describe the past fifty years as living life to the full. I have lived throughout these fifty years and sometimes, I was lived by them. But, hand on heart, or rather, one hand on your heart and one on your stomach, I would say that I had a great time and would do it all over again if I had the opportunity. I am still living my life to the full, as I always have, but that's how I like it. Anyone who knows me is aware that with me, work and fun go hand in hand.

Welcome to my story.
Welcome to my biotope.

Bart

BIOTOPE

*(Gr: βιος (bios) - life,
τοπος (topos) - place)*

is an area with a uniform landscape where specific organisms are able to thrive.

BIOTOPE

Welcome to Reet village

AND DON'T BE AFRAID TO GO ALL THE WAY DOWN TO THE BOTTOM!

In the 1960s a new priest arrived at the village of Reet, which, by the way, can be loosely translated as Bottom in all possible ways, shapes or forms. The nuns who ran the parish in those days wanted to welcome the new priest with open arms, so to speak. At the same time, they wanted to show what they, and the entire village, were made of. And so it came to pass that the church was adorned with a large banner sporting the slogan *'Welkom in ons Reet'*. This particular sense of humour, playful but at the same time provocative and perhaps a little bizarre, characterises the people from Reet. It is anchored in the heavy clay soil that is a hallmark of the village but you can see it pop up here, there and everywhere. It shines through in Bart's own creations and makes its muddy mark on Pastorale. Bart's work has grown from his roots in this village and this region. They just cannot be separated. Welcome to our Bottom.

WELKOM IN ONS REET
TE KOOP

Show us what you're made of

'IF YOU CAN'T CHANGE IT, EMBRACE IT.'

Pastorale is located in the village of Reet. A location with quite an unfortunate name, even more so as it is close to the neighbouring municipalities of Kontich and Aartselaar, all with their own connotations related to the lower extremities of the human body. You wouldn't be surprised to learn that this area is commonly known as the 'anal triangle'. And now, two options are open to you. You could move house and settle in a village with a less unusual name. Or you could make fun of your local village, take the p*** along with everybody else, and make the very best of it. Bart plumped for the second option and, literally as well figuratively, he went the whole way. In other words, he did the full Monty. Just take a good look at the Pastorale logo and consider what it means.
A lovely and shapely bare backside. A 'kont' as we like to call it in popular parlance. An ass, in other words. Designed as artistically as possible and avoiding vulgarity in any way, shape or form. This duality between a presbytery and a bare bottom works really well to create an interesting interaction, and, at the same time, it is a prime example of the basic sense of provocation and humour somehow dragged up from the clay of the village of Reet.

BURGH, PRESBYTERY, PASTORALE

Early 14th century. A pond, located above the hamlet of *Reeth* as it was known, close to Kontich, draws the attention of the Lord of Berckelaer, a vassal to the powerful dynasty of the knights of Berthout. He deems it the perfect location to build a farm. 'Het Hof' develops into the rural burgh of *Retergoed* that, in turn, will become the presbytery of Reet. Seven centuries on, this presbytery is at the heart of the multi-starred restaurant that has been blessed with the name of *Pastorale.*

FROM BOURG TO MEDIEVAL PRESBYTERY

The noble van Berckelaer family settles to the south of the 14th-century hamlet of *Reeth*, nearby Kontich and close to the springs that feed the Molenbeek, or Mill Stream. To strengthen his relationship with the clergy, whose powers are increasing, the Lord of Berckelaer commissions the building of two chapels in the corners of his *Retergoed* estate. One chapel is dedicated to Saint Mary Magdalene and will serve as the village church in later days. The other chapel is now known as the Laarkapel (Laar Chapel). In those days, the Retergoed estate with its rural burg and two chapels on the Laar is strongly anchored in the so-called social-residential relationship between the Church and the Court.

Before the year 1442 the van Berckelaer family makes a gift to the parish of this rural burgh with its gardens and fields. And so it came to pass that the burgh turned into a medieval presbytery, not far from the church. In the mid-15th century the church, with its new brick-built bell tower, takes up a prominent position in the new centre of the village of Reet.

FROM EARLY BAROQUE TO BUILDING A PRESBYTERY IN THE STYLE OF THE HIGH BAROQUE

In the 17th century the feudal *'curestede'* – the name then commonly used to denote a timber-framed parsonage – enjoyed the benefits of a brick tower, a thatched roof, two gardens, a walled arbour on a hill that was locally known as 'kneukelenberg' plus an orchard and two fields. The presbytery and its grounds undergo many changes. In 1661, at the rear of the old homestead, a detached longhouse is built. To the left of this, the parish priest commissions a new timber-framed presbytery, which will be erected between 1665 and 1668, the cost of which he bears himself.

When in 1714 – after the War of the Spanish Succession – knight Corneel vanden Branden

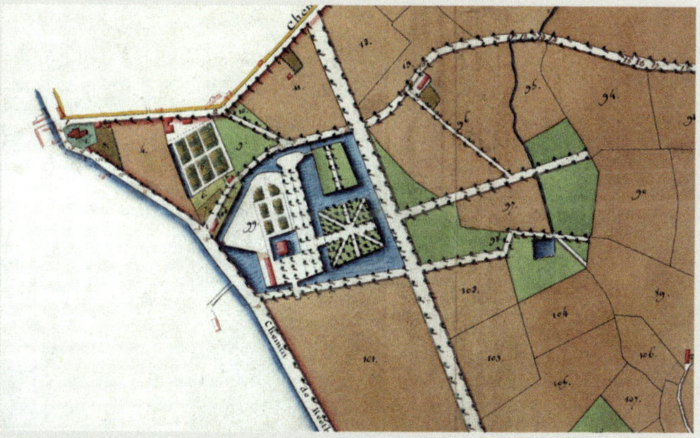

PRAETORIUM TOPARCHIAE DE REEDT, NEEFS, 1665, PUBLISHED IN 'NOTITIA MARCHIONATUS SACRI ROMANI IMPERII', JAQUES LE ROY, 1678, P. 244, CASTLE ARCHIVE REET.

PRIMITIVE LAND REGISTER 'COMMUNE DE REETH', SECTION C, 'DE LAER', NR. 9 AND 10, SURVEYOR ROGER, 1817 (LAND REGISTRY ARCHIVE ANTWERP). UNLIKE THE PRIVATE BUILDINGS (SHADED IN RED), THE CHURCH AND THE PRESBYTERY DISTINGUISH THEMSELVES AS RELIGIOUS BUILDINGS (SHADED IN DARK BLUE) FROM THE FOSSE OR POND, 'ET' FROM ETANG (LIGHT BLUE).

WEESEN, 1806 NATIONAL ARCHIVE ANTWERP

introduces the high baroque style to Laar Castle, the parish priest is brooding on his own expansion plans. He commissions a new brick-built wing to connect the existing, detached buildings to form a u-shaped presbytery. The new wing affords an axial perspective on the church and its ornate interior court.

In the wake of the French Revolution, in 1798, the high baroque presbytery is sealed off. It passes into the hands of the local authorities in 1799. Weesen's Atlas, printed in 1806 and thus pre-dating the Land Registry, shows this presbytery with its adjacent grounds including the 500-year-old foundations. After 1830, when Belgium gained independence, Reet presbytery started to decline and the topographical map drawn up by Philippe Vandermaelen in later years, 1844 to be precise, shows that the building had already been demolished.
This same map still shows the detached presbytery building with its timber cladding, dating all the way back to 1668. This now forms the heart of *Pastorale*.

THE LATE CLASSICIST PRESBYTERY

1831 is the year that Jozef Gaspar vanden Branden de Reeth, the owner of Laarhof, has a villa built at Rumstsestraat. This villa, named Bel Aria, was put up for sale in 1833. It was briefly considered as a suitable home for the parish priest, but in 1835 architect Ferdinand Berckmans, in the employ of the province of Antwerp, draws up the design for a new presbytery, the building that is now home to Pastorale. In 1839 – with great reluctance, having fought years of opposition – Berckmans finally submits his design for the two wings. To cut costs, the arched windows that formed part of his design have become rectangular and for the same reason, the roof is now covered in tiles instead of slate. The left wing will house the kitchen and the right wing will be used as a coach house. This Classicist style is reflected in the architecture of the presbytery through the use of horizontal lines and rectangular windows.
The elevated ground floor is the most important space in the house. The central hallway affords a perspective on the south-facing garden at the rear of the house and provides an element of symmetry. From here you can reach the cloakroom and, on the opposite side, on the right there is a large priest's office connected to the salon located right behind it. The dining room is located to the right and leads onto the kitchen in the side wing. A stone staircase gives access to the wine cellars and the pantry. Other floors can be reached via a wooden staircase.
We have been digging into 19th-century records and came up with building plans, building specifications, invoices and exchanges of correspondence between builders. We consulted many different sources, predominantly the National Archives but we also delved into records held at provincial and local levels. All of these demonstrate that the budget allowed by the municipality in the year 1835 was insufficient to implement the design by architect Ferdinand Berckmans to the letter. Major savings were made especially when it came to finishing off the interior decor. Nevertheless, once we had peeled away the various, more recent layers of

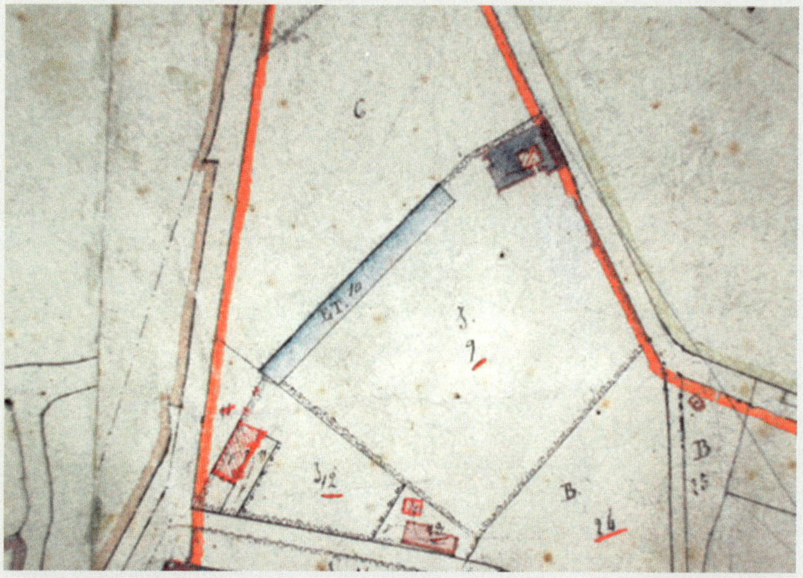

PRIMITIVE LAND REGISTER, SURVEYOR ROGER, 1817 (LAND REGISTRY ARCHIVE ANTWERP)

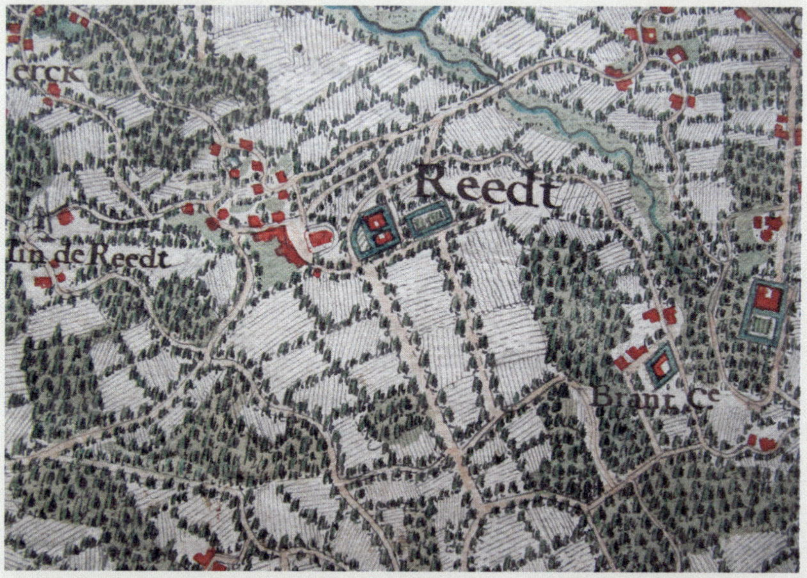

MILITARY MAP, NAUDIN LE JEUNE, 1726, (ARCHIVES MINISTÈRE DE L'ARMÉE DE TERRE, PARIS). PASTORALE IS LOCATED JUST ABOVE THE CASTLE WALL, BUT THE BUILDING IS NOT INDICATED ON THE MAP.

CABINET MAP, JOSEPH DE FERRARIS, 1778, (ROYAL LIBRARY BRUSSELS).

monochrome paint, recent research into the use of colours and materials confirmed the once sumptuous decor of the rooms, in a Classicist style with a hint of Empire. We also found that the ground floors were finished to a far higher standard than one might expect.

The presbytery built by Ferdinand Berckmans had a central axis which was built perpendicular to the Laarstraat. This central axis, typical for a semi-detached house, has since been restored and the grand hallway once again allows a view of the gardens at the rear of the property. The vestibule leads on to the spiral staircase, designed with pilasters and architraves in Empire style. The panelling is made of wood veneer and finished by a wood veneer plinth intersected with marbled, ruby-red (*rouge royal)* panels. Turn the eye upwards and notice that the walls are covered in green paint with a cream-coloured corniche to create an illusion, or trompe l'œil. Unfortunately, as the house has undergone many refurbishments, not much remains of these original decorative elements. Panelling, walls and corniches have since been painted over in new colours, in a predominantly green and black colour scheme. When they started to restore the building, the craftsmen (employed by Bart) made sure that any layers worth preserving were only given a very light clean. They then covered anything they wanted to keep with a professional coating to ensure that the past could be brought back to life. Last but not least, the original smooth limestone floor, made up of 40 x 40 cm tiles with the deepest anthracite colour, was restored to its full shine and splendour. In the salon, there are still patches of wallpaper with stylised floral patterns on a white background. The outline of the flowers is printed in gold. The mantelpiece was plastered over in a previous era. When attempts were made to restore it to its former glory, decorative paintings in 'empire' colours were found on the surround. This colour scheme is Napoleonic in nature rather than religious. As such, it is quite remarkable to come across these colours in what is after all a religious building. The mantelpiece itself is made of *vert de mer,* a black marble interspersed with green. In the lower part of the hearth, the orange-veined *napoleon rouge* panels are displaying the splendour they had all these years ago. The white-veined marble has been buffed to a shine, so much so that you get the illusion of depth. The bottom of the hearth is inlaid with diamond-shaped, white and black-green tiles within a setting of the same colour. The local craftsmen have made a superb job of restoring its former glory and turning it into a focal point once again. And, to top it all off, the chimney is now clad in mirrored glass to provide a contemporary accent.

FROM LOCAL PARSONAGE TO PASTORALE

At the end of the last century the presbytery starts to crumble for lack of proper maintenance. In 1991 the presbytery gardens are divided into building plots. On the edge of the gardens a new presbytery is erected along with private housing. The local authority commissions a municipal park. The presbytery, which has preserved some of its Classicist style, finds a new use: it is turned into a restaurant.

In 1992 Bart De Pooter grabs the opportunity to set up shop in this presbytery that was in danger of losing its Classicist looks. A new creative wind blows across this historic domain.

ABOVE: FRONT VIEW, F. BERCKMANS, 1835, PROVINCIAL ARCHIVE ANTWERP.

BELOW: THE RENOVATION INTO A RESTAURANT, 1991.

HOME

Past
oral
e-motions

Taking the past as a starting point, comprising the history of our building but also the history of our own, Burgundian, dining culture, we create tastes that touch our senses to culminate in emotions, experiences.

ORAL
F

BART: Really, even after all these years it feels like I only have temporary custody of this building. I am just an itinerant who spends a little time here, looks after the building and hands it on when the time has come. With Pastorale we have created a new identity for this building, but we have also re-invigorated it. It has always been our ultimate ambition to return the presbytery to what it is: a resplendent edifice; also, to give it a soul and a value without affecting the history and all of the different elements that make it so unique. Plenty of clergymen have gone before me: so far, I have counted over thirty priests and chaplains. Speaking for myself, I cannot claim to be a saint. Far from it. Nevertheless, this building is not trying to commit blasphemy. Or, perhaps, just a little.

Carlo Mistiaen 2003

Napkins laughing at one another is a work of art by Carlo Mistiaen. It is, in fact, an installation of coffee cups and Bruges lace. The materials were lifted out of their culinary context and rearranged to form two skulls having a chat. This 'kaffee klatsch' or chat over a cuppa, has definitely taken on a different dimension.

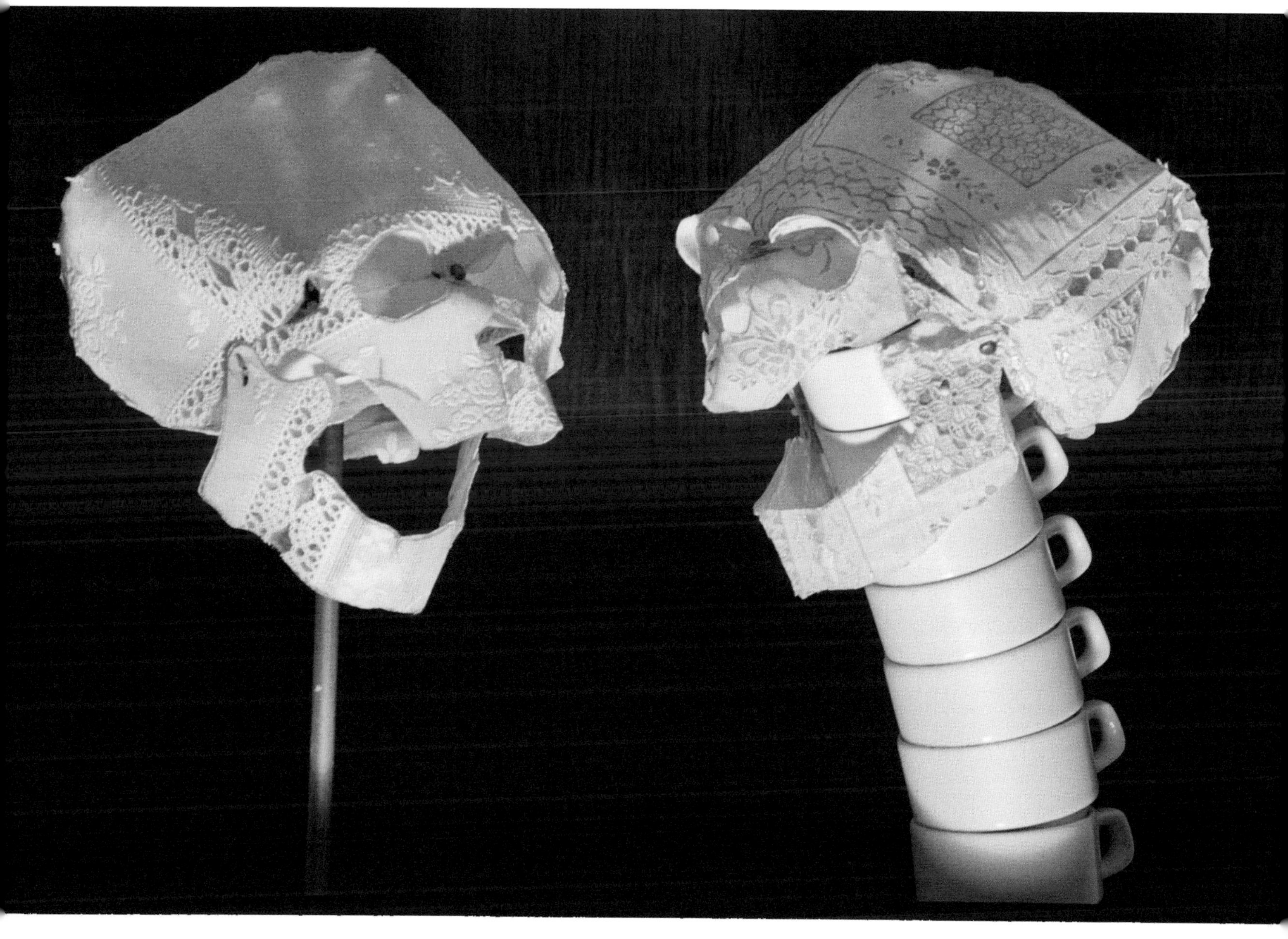

BART: Oh well, it's never easy to start out. For anyone. As a fourteen-year-old pupil of St. Rita's College in Kontich, reading and writing did not come easy to me. They very kindly asked me to leave. Naturally I was then on the lookout for an occupation that suited me better.
Working as a weekend waiter quite appealed to me. I remember clearly that they gave me the job and that, at the door, the boss asked me: 'Wait a second, how old are you?' I was quite tall for my age, but I did own up: I was only fourteen years old. And so, this job passed me by. A few months later, I tried again to get my foot in the door. They didn't even recognise me and on this occasion, I lied through my teeth and said I was sixteen years old. Success! They asked me to start that coming Saturday.

And then, after I had learnt the basics, I had the great good fortune to be hired by Pierre Romeyer from Maison de Bouche at Hoeilaart, then a leading three-star restaurant. Pierre was like a father to me. He used products of the highest quality, had a great eye for detail and knew exactly how to prepare all of the different ingredients. In me, he spotted a youngster full of motivation and drive. Totally willing to give it a go. One fine day I was put in charge of the fish section. I seized my opportunity and never left my own particular fish 'counter' until I was drafted into the Army. Under Romeyer, and after only one year in the kitchen, I was awarded the title of Belgium's best junior chef.

MAMA TO BART - MARIA MERTENS

I wasn't there when he was stirring the pots and pans for the first time. When I came out of the washroom early in the morning, I heard the clatter of cutlery and crockery in the kitchen. And, at the table, there was Bart who was just finishing off his bowl of porridge. The saucepan he had used for his porridge was sitting on the stove. Bart was only four years old and had managed to do it all by himself. From lighting the fire to making a yummy porridge. I think that, even at that age, he spent about half of his time in the kitchen. The other half he could be found in the vegetable garden. And this is where he developed his taste palate. After all, that's how it works. Once you have discovered the taste of fresh peas, frozen peas make a very poor substitute.

At the age of five he told us he was not happy with frozen peas and asparagus soup from a packet. And of course, this would usually happen at family celebrations. He would have one mouthful before telling everyone, without any hesitation whatsoever, that they had cooked with frozen food. And then he went on to tell these people, who had gone to the effort of bringing a dish, why things were better at home.

One day, when he told me that he wanted to train as a chef, at first I found it hard to believe him. I didn't even know that there were schools for that. I worked as a cook at a primary school. But, that you could actually go back to the classroom and train to be a professional chef – that was a completely new idea to me.

At any rate, we wanted Bart to take up this opportunity if this was what his heart was set on. And so we went to various chef's schools all around the country in search of the one best suited to Bart. We went for PIVA in Antwerp.
I have to admit that this is not really what I had in mind for Bart. I still don't think that being a chef is a proper job. But, seeing how this gave Bart a new spring in his step, I can only conclude that after all it was the right decision for him. Even though, up to this day, I still don't know which made him happier: the opportunity to cook or just the fact that he had to spend less time with his textbooks *(said with a wink).*

Soon after Bart got his diploma, he had the opportunity to establish something lovely and very close to home: Pastorale. Even then I was sure that Bart would make his mark. He had a great idea and the energy to make it work.
But, on the first day of opening, things went slightly haywire. Bart was in the kitchen with only one other chef and there was an endless stream of customers. He did not want to turn anyone away and so he called me to tell me that he was in a pickle, so to speak. I came over to help him out. I only did one shift but it lasted for ten years. I was able to stand the pace until I was sixty and then I threw the towel in the ring.

I used to be in charge of my own kitchen, but it was Bart who wielded the spoon at Pastorale. He was harder on me than on anyone else. He quite literally told me: 'Yes, but that is the way things should be. Everyone else is here on a temporary basis but you will always be here. And that's why I have to be harder on you.'
When all is said and done, we worked very well together. A kitchen tandem that cycled quite smoothly through the shifts. At least, in the beginning. But, if you're working in a restaurant that aims for the stars, you have to give the very best of yourself over and over again. No matter if you are twenty years young or won't see fifty again. Every single day I threw myself into the business for the full one hundred percent. From 7 o'clock in the morning until midnight.
My specialty was patisserie and 'the cold side' as it is known: cold dishes and garnishes. Every morning, without fail, I transformed six kilos of flour into bread rolls. Not a job for the faint-hearted.

When the restaurant is open and customers are having their meals, Bart is calm personified. I have seen him lose his rag only once with a member of his team. This was when Michelin were in the dining room. We had just launched a new menu that included the very first asparagus of the season. Fantastically tasty but most of the new crop had arrived with green tips. And, at this level, asparagus must be a virginal white in colour. The very few white asparagus we had were carefully put aside for the Michelin man. Everything went according to plan until one of the waiters decided to put the plate with the beautifully white asparagus... on the wrong table. It wasn't long before a bowl of butter sauce went flying through the Pastorale kitchen. This was a one-off outburst and Bart regretted it immediately.

Cooking is truly in his blood. It runs in the family. From time to time I have found it quite difficult to deal with, but I am also incredibly proud that he has found his own way and comes up with all those great projects. Clearly, he is his mother's child.

OPENING PASTORALE OCTOBER 1993

BART: The presbytery had been vacant for ten years when I started out here as a chef in 1992. The local business community considered this building to be a splendid location for a Michelin-starred restaurant. Even though I was only just a spring chicken, occasionally I made the headlines. Up to a point, I have my creativity to thank for that, but persistence comes into it as well. Or it could be down to my good looks? Who knows? Whatever. At any rate, these entrepreneurs knew whom they were dealing with and saw me as their future chef. My boss at the time was Firmin De Vogel of Restaurant Paddock. I really enjoyed working for him. Firmin's advice to me was to demand a high salary. With the idea in mind that they would never agree, which meant that I would carry on working for him. Well, I duly attended the interview and, as we all know, life can have some surprises in store.
And then some more.
They said Yes. I was left at a complete loss as to what to say, but very quickly realised that there's no time like the present to prove myself. I took over the business in 1993. One month later, I asked Jan (Bleys) to sort out the gardens.

JAN: Bart was customer number 26. From the very first time, we felt that we were kindred spirits and this feeling of kinship has remained up to this day. I don't like to exaggerate, but I can say with confidence that either Pastorale or my own business would not be what they are now if we had not met at that particular point in time. For me, back then, Pastorale was a prestige project. A project that does not land in your lap every day. In fact, Bart gave me my own platform, literally and figuratively, so I could show my mettle. All we did to start off with was to remove an ugly patch of land and get rid of the white gravel in the front garden, but we soon got started on the interior design. We made some small tweaks here and there, as we were getting deeper into the project, we decided to stop tinkering and approach the work on a larger scale. We looked into the history of the building, investigated its heritage, examined the walls and delved into the archives. Each tiny little change was weighed up very carefully. For example, the ceiling was adorned with verses from Virgil's Bucolics, composed in the first century BC.
In this work, the poet describes a pastoral, idyllic Eden where the entire focus is on enjoyment. In the same way that the Gardens of Eden knew no seasons, Bart's cooking goes above and beyond routine. His creations never lack harmony, but he literally and figuratively adds a touch of salt to Virgil's sweet elements. That's Bart for you. He's had this playful streak from a young age and (fortunately) it has never left him.

In 1994 the building was included in the Register of Listed Buildings as the *Presbytery of the Parish of Saint Mary Magdalene,* based on its value for architectural history.

O lovely boy, come here:
see the Nymphs bring for you,
lilies in heaped baskets:
the bright Naiad picks, for you
pale violets
and the heads of poppy flowers,
blends narcissi
with fragrant fennel flowers:
then, mixing them with spurge laurel
and more sweet herbs,
embroiders hyacinths
with yellow marigolds.
I'll gather quinces, pale with soft down
and chestnuts, that my Amaryllis loved:
Someone is adding waxy plums:
they too shall be honoured:
and Bart adds a pinch of salt
and I'll pluck you, O laurels, and you,
neighbouring myrtle,
since, so placed, you mingle
your sweet perfumes.

The renovation of the interior

BART: The interior of the building was just so kitsch! We improved it no end just by removing disruptive elements. We found a complete hotchpotch of cabinets from furniture warehouses, plastic angels on the wall, pink curtains, swinging doors, a red floor and ugly shades of brown pretty much eee-very-where. Every item we removed increased the number of people who came through the door. The emptier the decor, the fuller the restaurant. After a while I started to wonder whether we ought to chuck out our chairs and tables as well. So, the first stage of the renovation was an austerity drive. In the second phase we involved artists that elevated these premises onto a higher plane. We wanted to give them a platform. All of the artists with whom we have worked, up to this day, have made a contribution to our identity. They helped us to establish Pastorale and make it into what it is today.
JAN: For me, Pastorale mainly grew from gut feeling. Both Bart and I are very much aware of where we started from and where we want to go. We quickly get the sense of a particular artwork: does it fit in or is it going to clash?
Just take a look at the art videos that are playing on a continuous loop on the walls of the building. They have come a long way. At one point Bart threw in the towel.
BART: Yes, you lost me there for a bit *(laughs)*.
JAN: I had a quiet chat with Arno De Pooter, the video artist. And all of a sudden, within an hour, he had created a masterpiece. Sometimes you just know that they've got it in them. And then you have to shake the tree a little to get it out. If you take a look around Pastorale then you will see art videos on every wall. Astonishing images, quite unsettling sometimes, but always great to look at. I am still glad that we have continued to push this young artist and most importantly – that we never stopped believing in his work.

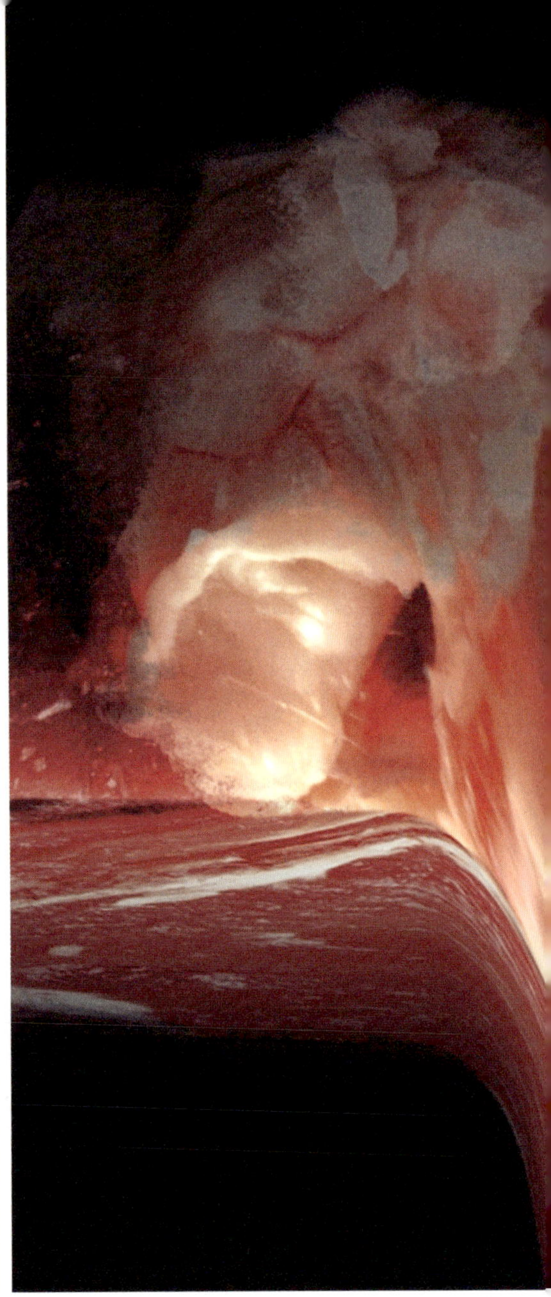

Arno De Pooter

ARNO: Jan and I had been friends for a while when he introduced me to Bart De Pooter. Not because we have the same surname and he wanted to check if I was an illegitimate child, but because he felt that my conceptual vision was of interest to Pastorale.

I was simply overwhelmed when I first came to Pastorale. First of all you're blown away by the art on display and then, slowly but surely, you start to see the bigger picture. A constantly evolving interior. To my huge amazement, at my first brainstorming session I was invited to share the table and enjoy what was on the menu. Just one tiny detail: I had just eaten dinner at home. At this first session we discussed some drafts, sketched out some initial ideas and went through all of the possibilities. My first impression of Bart was that he was somewhat reserved, but once we started talking about the creative aspect, I discovered a completely different side to him.

We have gone through numerous drafts. Also, on occasion we drew up more detailed plans before we decided not to use them. But all of a sudden, all of the pieces of the jigsaw just fell into place. We decided to dissect the menu so to speak, reassemble the ingredients and reinforce them in an original, very visual way by showing them on the screens in the restaurant. This takes the dining experience to an even higher plane. Using static images would have been too easy and too obvious and

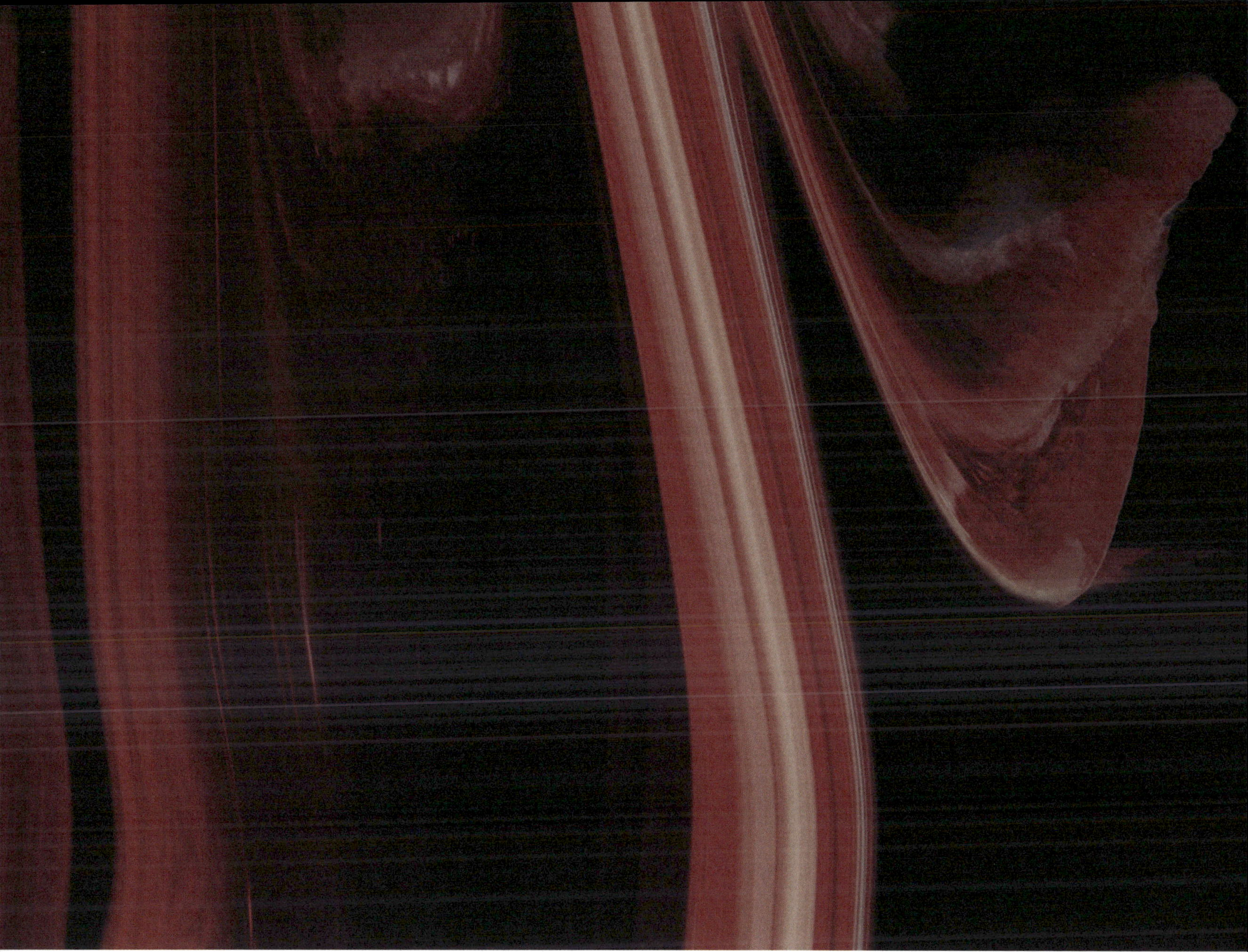

so we decided to go for fascinating, moving images of food. Images that invite you to look at them. It has to be said that we always started off with static images but we then played around with them.
The project took five months from start to finish. In more detail, we spent four months on searching and researching and then it took one month to implement it all. Towards the end I really went for it. I did some more research; went to the clay pits; took a huge amount of photographs. All of a sudden the process had drawn me in completely and I fell under the spell of the quest for the perfect images. But even so, where Bart and Jan were concerned, the whole thing was still too mainstream. They wanted to be even more daring. I had to explore the boundaries of what could be done and what was really not done in a restaurant like Pastorale. And so I went off in search of images that showed blood spurting out, or for universes that were self-sufficient and made in such a way that you always wanted to drown yourself in them.
When the project was ready to deliver, I wasn't 100% convinced myself that it would work. I was happy with my own contribution but I had not yet viewed the entire picture. When, a few months later, I enjoyed dinner at Pastorale, in that amazing setting, and tasted that great food accompanied by those images, I knew that after all it had all been worthwhile. Everything fell into place. When I think back to that moment I still get goose pimples.

BART: So many young people flock to Pastorale. All of them, without exception, experience a huge amount of growth. I am not just talking about artists – that is a given – but it also goes for our kitchen chefs. At Pastorale we give them plenty of opportunities to grow. I have often met parents who wanted to thank me in person. Yes, I have played a role in this, but more importantly, so has the entire team. Credit where credit is due. Pastorale is not just Bart De Pooter. Pastorale is an entire team comprised of people that, on an individual basis, are very good at what they do, but are totally committed to working as a team and want to do better every single day. There is a slogan above the kitchen extractor that is a beautiful summary of our attitude:

ONE TEAM.
ONE PHILOSOPHY.
ONE TARGET.

CHEF OF THE YEAR In 2012 Bart achieved marks of 18/20 in the Gault Millau culinary guide, a score that had never been achieved before. This accreditation is based on his aesthetic drive and his respect for the product. Nevertheless, a chef is only as good as his team. Therefore, Bart refuses to be the only player in the video that is made of him. He decides to cut pictures of his team members into long strips to form a type of super-human.

ONE PHILOSOPHY ONE TARGET

Bart is obstinate. Like a donkey.
But far from stupid.
– JAN BLEYS-

A work in progress

The designers faced a huge challenge: how to establish a dialogue between the past and the present. The design team did not carry out a reconstruction per se; rather, it 'clad' the room in a way that was historically sound, but also introduced its own contemporary touches, shades and colours. After all, Pastorale makes its own way in the world. This is a major part of its identity and it wants to be a trend-setter in designing its indoor and outdoor areas to exude gastronomy in every way possible. This *work in progress*, as the name implies, is evolving all the time but it is never less than totally alive and kicking to create a total project aimed at the Fluxus of our times. This very continuity ensures a coherence between meals and recipes and the interior and exterior decoration of your home. The confluence of art in general support this concept. Pastorale has turned into a very hospitable venue which has gone far beyond the mere enjoyment of the lovely dishes that are placed in front of you at your very own table. Pastorale can be described as a culinary mansion. Enter at your peril. But when you make the effort, the rewards are high. The craftiness and craftsmanship hidden behind its nooks and crannies is not apparent at first glance. It has to be discovered to be appreciated. But, once you get the hang of it, you will love the experience, from the food you are enjoying, through to the plate on which it is served, right down to the painted wooden beams supporting the roof. Craft elevated into art. Open your mind and look around you. This is the only way to discover it all.

SHRIMP - SALTY PLANTS AT THE NORTH SEA >

PAST
ORAL
E MOTIONS 2011 Pastorale needs no introduction. Nevertheless, one was produced in 2011. In just under three minutes, this video completely draws you into the world of Bart and Pastorale. Surprising and provocative, featuring art, dishes, eating with your hands and playing with the senses. Everything is shown and nothing is spared. Fast-changing images of the sometimes back-breaking work in the kitchen are interspersed with images of works of art and pictures of a young woman who is swept away by the type of sensual restaurant experience that can only be the stuff of her dreams.

BART: At Pastorale everything is based on what's on your plate. On our own philosophy of cooking. Everything else will fall into place. Part of our philosophy is to steer clear of the well-trodden paths. First and foremost, I want to create my own brand and follow my own 'gut feel'. A chef tends to have a well-developed instinct. Friends have been heard calling me 'obstinate', which I will then obstinately deny. Ever since I started to do my own thing in my own obstinate way, I have created a clear platform for myself, gained my first star, and acted as a consultant on a variety of projects. The only way I can grow is through others. I am reassured by the fact that I am also capable of nurturing the growth of people, brands and companies thanks to the expertise I have gathered over the years.

Occasionally I can be a bit too obstinate, or stubborn, for my own good. Then, I bang my head against the wall. But, all you get is a bump on the head and that heals easily. I will always listen to what the people around me have to say. I am grateful to anyone who gives me feedback. But there comes a time where you just have to make our own decisions, go your own way and to hell with the consequences. Our tables are a great example.

We wanted a non-static table that could be adjusted to the dish we were serving. Food always evolves and we wanted to be prepared for that. Of course, we did not want to turn our restaurant into a theme park; it had to have a certain finesse. All well and good, but how do you approach this? How do you create an interactive experience with a static concept like a table?

Right from the start, we selected tables with an organic design, with inlays made from six different materials: leather, marble, bronze, brass, silver and porcelain. You can link them together in any way you like to create long, amorphous party tables. You can remove a few elements to put in a coal-fired grill for example, or candles with a special significance or else an arch that you can hang small dishes on. The marquetry effect can also be used to incorporate a plate, salt and pepper cellars or whatever you like, really. In other words, the table is a direct extension of the plate and aims to blur the edges between the plate and your dining experience.
JAN: I'll have you know, we spent 18 months working on those tables. We slaved away at them and it took a team of four designers. These tables were never quite right. Sometimes they were not fluid enough, or they did not fit in with the philosophy, or they were just plain ugly.
BART: I was never ever happy. And one night I got really wound up. Angry with the situation but also with the others. So I picked up a pencil...
JAN: *(laughing)* ... and he threw it at me. He said: "Go on then, just do it yourself. You seem to know best."
I picked up that pencil. And made a start. Oh well, we are still good friends, same as before *(said with a wink)*.

Everything flowed from our philosophy. Not based on any particular model or way of building. No, our philosophy took centre stage. Based on nature, on organic shapes. This is how we created our tables and that's what makes them unique. We used sustainable natural materials that were used to craft our tables by hand, piece by piece, in the artisan way.

My home. My house.
My stilthouse. 2008

For *My house*, created by Arne Quinze, they really went the extra mile. To create this project, part of the restaurant was stripped down completely. The ceiling was adjusted and all of the radiators were removed. The restaurant closed down for a total of twenty days, three of which were spent by Arne to work on his sculpture, before it was revealed at the grand opening.
The artist was given carte blanche and magically transformed Pastorale into his own personal atelier, where he produced an installation with wooden slats, some of which were painted in a fluorescent orange. With this installation made of wood, Arne Quinze, the artist, connects the various dining rooms that are all on the same floor, engages in a dialogue with other floors and melts them into one single whole. The numbers on the slats personify addresses and the lattice structure symbolises the virtual connections between these addresses: a symbolic internet, as it were, that connects things.
With this work of art, Quinze has primarily strengthened several elements that were already present: feeling at home, transparency, working with shadows, the use of natural materials, wood in various colours and of various thicknesses. Transparency, tension, a variety of textures... All of these are components that are essential to the creation of a good dish. This is why this work fits perfectly within the concept of Pastorale.

MY HOUSE - Bart's signature is the interaction between art and kitchen. He never concealed his great love for art and architecture. On the contrary. It even gets a prominent place in his restaurant.

A wall of glass

MARTIJN DEDECKER – INTERIOR DESIGNER We departed from the story of a biotope, of nature. For reference images we looked into various types of moss and mould so we could remain within the natural world and the patterns it creates. Moss and mould are living organisms that evolve continuously, are moving all the time and adapt to their environment. Just like Pastorale and just like Bart. Using this as our basis, we started the search for a way, a technique to reproduce these mosses and moulds, through the medium of glass as well as paint, to make them look as true to nature as possible. Each glass panel was made by hand to make sure that the patterns form a beautiful continuation from one panel to the next. We had to negotiate quite a few hurdles along the way. We produced around forty samples before we had one that we could work with. The right colour, the perfect pattern. It all had to come together.

As everything was hand-crafted, we had to start over several times. Using this technique, there were some reactions we had not anticipated and we did not know how it would affect the project.

If I am asked to describe my collaboration with Bart in one single word, I would use the term 'challenging'. Bart knows very well how to push people to go the extra mile; just that little bit further than they had in mind. He tries to get the most out of everybody by questioning everything. And to be honest, that can be a great thing to do. This is how you rise above yourself and create unique objects.

Atelier Vierkant 2016

The pots on display in the restaurant constitute an entire collection, created by Atelier Vierkant. These pots can be seen nowhere else in the world.
After brief stops in New York, Madrid and Singapore they are now on display in Reet and will not travel again. The pots are made for outdoor use but they also look great indoors and, in fact, they make a bigger impression in their current location. The structure of the pots is in complete harmony with Pastorale's culinary philosophy. Moreover, they fit perfectly with the tables and the other elements of the interior design.

Kirsten Spuijbroek 2017

If Bart ever happens to find himself in a comfort zone, he wants to leave it straight away. But, and this is my honest opinion, what Bart enjoys even more is to push other people out of their comfort zone. The porcelain flowers placed on the table are a prime example. Artist Kirsten Spuijbroek works in partnership with Martijn Dedecker to design and produce these tiny works of art that should not be underestimated in any way, shape or form. It would surprise you to know that underneath all that delicate porcelain lingers a flower that was once living and breathing. These flowers, crafted with much love and attention to detail, were steeped in a bath to give them their manifold layers that turned them into porcelain flowers.

VIOLET POTATOES COOKED WITH HAY >

Flower urns in the garden
1800 kg of clay – 6 months 2017

In keeping with the restaurant, the garden was also enhanced by inspirational works created by contemporary artists. From two monumental terracotta urns Bart takes his pick of edible plants and before long, their aroma will set your taste buds alight in one of Bart's culinary creations.

These garden urns are of an entirely different calibre compared to the other vases and pots on display in Pastorale. These two massive garden urns took six months to produce and, all in all, required 1800 kg of clay. This clay had to be applied in just the right way and each layer had to dry out before going into the oven to prevent cracks. A great feat of craftsmanship resulting in a simply splendid urn. However, the Pastorale gardens are so much more than 'just' two urns.

GARDEN APRIL 1993

A contemporary garden

After the refurbishment, the original proportions of the garden turned out to be all wrong for the building. The building's small perimeter wall did not do justice, or any favours, to the original grandeur of the building in any way whatsoever. In the autumn of 1995 the gardens underwent a radical redesign. They would serve as a green, open-air dining area. This design has stood the test of time and, to this day, forms a beautiful complement to the 19th-century, classical architecture of the building itself. Even more, it enhances the look of the restaurant owned by this top chef. The ingredients used to create the pattern have much in common with the classic French art of garden design: areas laid to lawn, gravel paths, topiary bushes as well as shrubs that are allowed to grow almost wild. The plans for the garden echo the plans of the house. In the same way that the house appears to be symmetrical but isn't really, the garden is now once again planned around a central axis that reflects the design of the formal flower beds. The gardens at the rear are, just as before, enclosed by rigourously clipped hornbeam trees, but can be viewed from the windows. A little bower, perfect for lovers, affords a glimpse of the Astrid Park that borders onto the rear of the property.

Taking up the baton from space 2010

BART: The garden sculpture was made by Dirk Frimout and bears the name of *The astronaut who conducts the sea*. Dirk was a pioneer, the first Belgian in space. For me, this statue represents my own role as a trailblazer in the culinary world. But, it also stands for conducting and delegating from a distance. Pastorale is my home where I feel safe and it is also where everything began, but now and again I feel the need to spread my wings, to set foot outside the four walls of my kitchen and to make something else happen. Finally, this statue, for me, also represents globalisation. I manage the team remotely, delegate tasks from a distance and this allows me to take up this pioneering role. Yes, I am ready to be *that* Belgian who takes up the baton of gastronomy and runs with it. Not only in my own country - I am also planning to go across borders.

TAKE UP THE PIONEER'S ROLE BY EXPLORING, UNDERSTANDING OTHER CULTURES AND UNDERTAKING UNIQUE PROJECTS. NOT JUST IN YOUR OWN COUNTRY BUT ALSO ABROAD.

The man who laughs and cries 2009

For the front garden we opted for Portuguese laurel hedges. In our, now narrowed, garden we used these to counteract the pronounced contours created by the widening of the road and restore the optical distance to the house. Also, they emphasise the horizontal lines contained in the façade and support the side beams. On the left hand side, the clipped laurel is used to envelop a plinth that supports a bust, dating back to the interbellum, of the luscious Queen Astrid, the grandmother of our current King Phillip. And in the meantime, Fabre's laughing man makes everyone feel welcome.

BART: The first statue that Jan Fabre installed in the gardens of Pastorale was entitled *De man die huilt en lacht*. In other words, the man who cries and laughs (at the same time). This is a very ambivalent statue and very typical of the artist. Or, to put it more precisely, it shows the naked character of the artist. With his hands he holds a book with the title: *'Je suis un erreur'*. Grammatically speaking, this should be *'une erreur'*. Look at it for as long as you like, it is well nigh impossible to read the expression on his face. I identify very much with this sculpture as it is about acquiring knowledge, doing the unexpected, going deep. Sometimes I reach depths that almost make me cry. On the other hand, it gives me a great deal of pleasure to make things happen. Which puts a big smile on my face. You fall down and you dust yourself off again. You laugh and you cry. And, all the time, with both naked feet firmly planted on the ground.

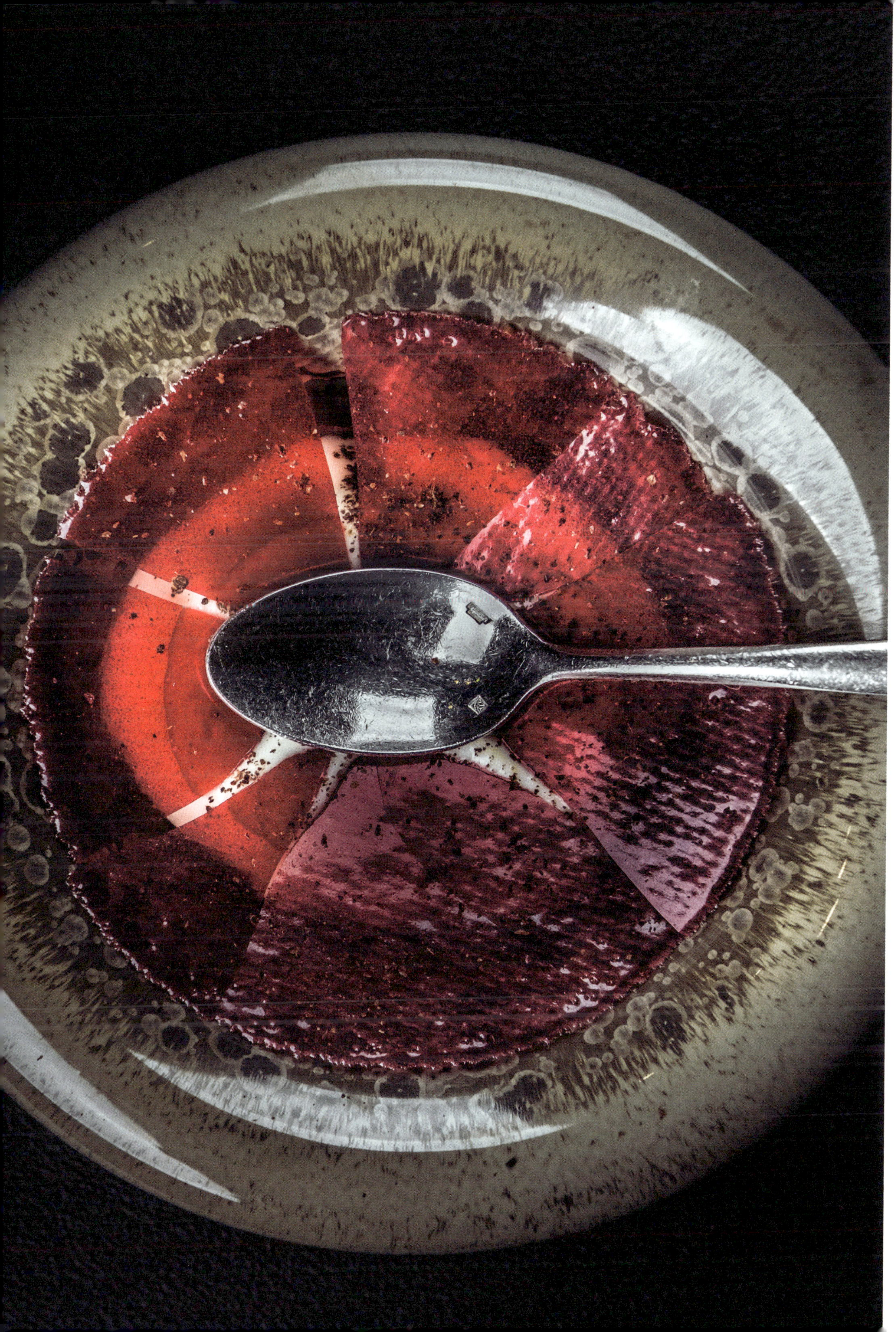

HIT ME

POTATO

CASSIS BERRY

TARRAGON

At lonely heights

Just at the back of the gardens of the parsonage, there is a small hill. It is not a work of art by any means, but for the local priest, it must have been of immense value. After all, from his elevated position on the hill, he would have been able to keep an eye on any villager passing through the village by way of the road. And act accordingly if he saw anything in any way suspicious.

Oh well, the surrounding hedges and the entrance gate are no more. They have faded into obscurity. There is no reason whatsoever to believe that Pastorale will ever feel the need to restore this ancient custom of the clergy. The only reason Bart now climbs this tiny bump in the landscape is to take an iconic picture or two.

TRUFFLE - DARK BEER - COTTAGE CHEESE - OXALIS

TERRINE OF FOIE GRAS - RED CHICORY - PECAN NUT - CEDAR WOOD

'Bart De Pooter and his team connect the world they live in with the microcosm of the forest, the infinity of the ocean and the riches of the field.'

Perusing the menu at Pastorale, your eye falls on this message. At a single glance you find out all you need to know about the philosophy of Pastorale. This philosophy centres around one single word: Biotope.

Bart started to work out this philosophy as long ago as 2007. Eventually it took ten years before the first menu landed on the tables at Pastorale. On the one hand, the philosophy had to be fine-tuned, and this took time, but on the other hand people were not yet ready for it. It's all well and good being a pioneer and being ahead of your time, but if you introduce your concept too early and people don't want to jump aboard, you yourself may miss the boat altogether. And this is precisely why Bart kept his philosophy to himself for a bit before introducing it to the wider world. Every menu compiled since 2017 is based on this principle.
The philosophy is given its external expression by the 'Menu Flora', which consists of a series of vegetarian dishes. Although the menu is complete by itself, guests are able to complement the 'Flora' menu with fish ('Menu Aqua') or meat ('Menu Fauna'). The culmination is to combine both menus to create 'Menu Biotoop'.

BART: Already in 2008 I wanted to introduce a biotope, but I was still misunderstood. At that time, the experience, not nature, was central to the gastronomic world. But because I increasingly used organic forms in my restaurant, I felt confident that the story of biotope could work. Slowly but surely, the whole thing started to work and blend together. It became a whole that still stands today.
Biotope actually starts from different worlds that occur in the same environment. Take the pheasant. It eats cereals, oats, corn. If you combine those with one another, together with the flowers the pheasant has walked between, you just feel that it's right.

SEA URCHIN - MUSSEL - COCKLE - FENNEL RISOTTO - YUZU - ALGAE >

THIS DISH IS A GOOD EXAMPLE OF A BIOTOPE. EVERYTHING IS TAKEN FROM THE SEA AND WELDED INTO A COHERENT WHOLE. NOT JUST BY THE COMBINATION OF MUSSELS WITH COCKLES AND SEA URCHIN, BUT ALSO, AND ESPECIALLY, BY ADDING BEAUTIFUL SILT PLANTS AND ALGAE TO THE MIX. TOGETHER WITH A MERINGUE OF PLANKTON, IT FORMS ITS OWN TINY BIOTOPE.

Clay bread

The clay bread from Reet and its surrounding area is famous around the world. We are referring to *Kleibrood*, the name popularly used in the area for the flat, oval lumps, shaped much like a turnip, that are formed naturally in the Rupelian clay. When young, they tend to look like a round artisan farmer's bread with a fine dusting of flour. These clay breads can grow into huge limestone banks. 'Clay breads' are typical for this region but they are also found in Madagascar, the USA, New Zealand, Australia, Canada, Spain and England.
They are known by their scientific name of *Septaria*. Made into jewellery, they are reputed to form a spiritual bridge between your own true self and Mother Earth. Bart has put this Rupelian gemstone to good use by commissioning authentic-looking plates on which refined finger food is served.

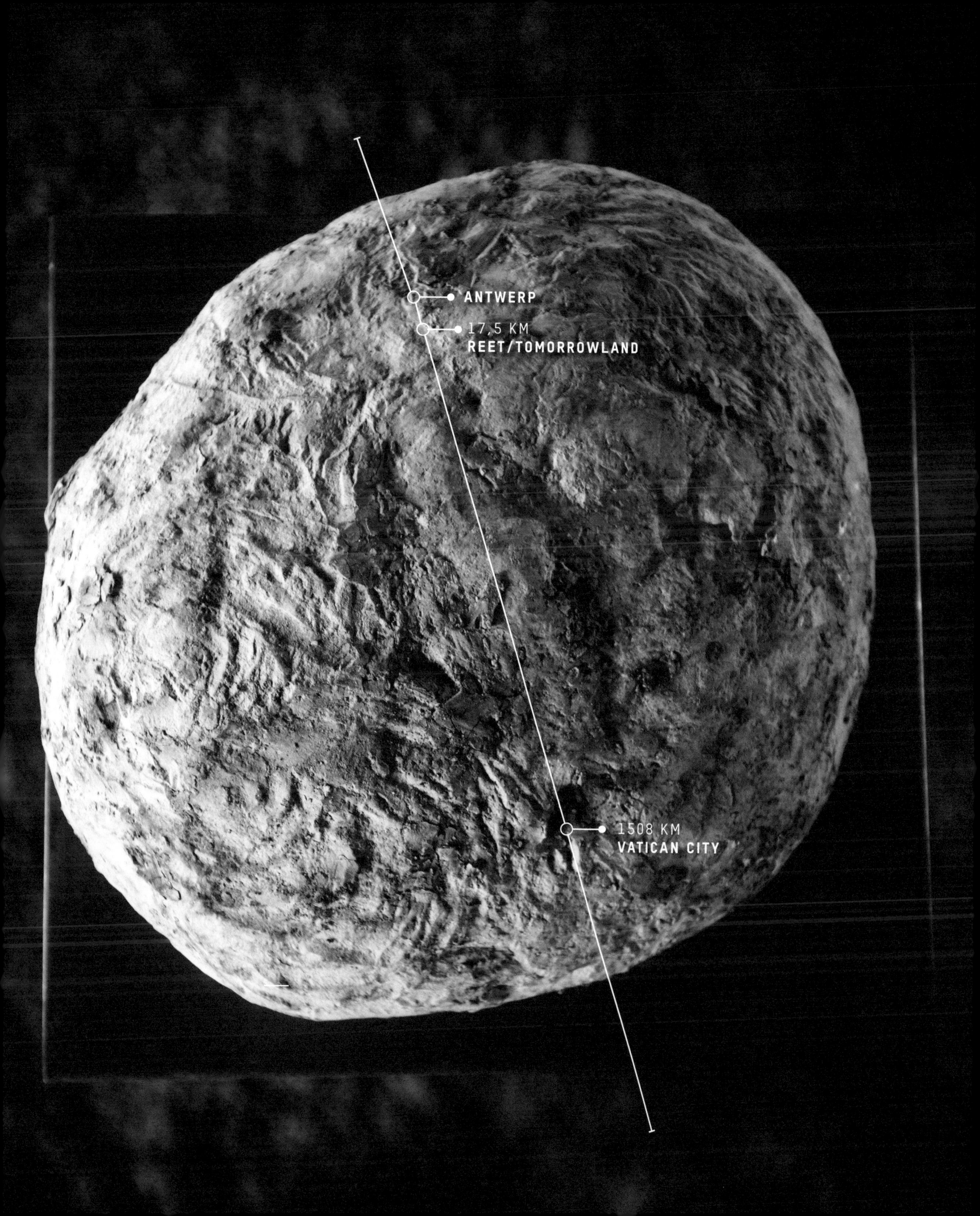
ANTWERP
17,5 KM
REET/TOMORROWLAND
1508 KM
VATICAN CITY

From clay bread to gilded stone

BART: Ever since I first started out as a chef I have liked eating with my hands. It brings you closer to your food and gives you a great first impression of what your food will taste like. And this is why I like to start off the menu with finger food and conclude it in the same way. The finger food I serve as a first course always entails a walk around the gardens. The food itself is served on clay breads from Reet to establish an instant connection with the locale. Not only do I use this type of earthenware breads because it looks beautiful, but also because the local element, or terroir, is gaining ground all the time. You can't be any more local than by working with a piece of clay that has been anchored in the local soil for millions of years. And these stones still contain fossilised water. That is unique. It can only happen here. And that's why we went back to basics by presenting all of our finger food on a locally made plate. A plate that cannot be claimed by anyone who is not a 'Retenaar' – born and bred in Reet. The meal is brought to a close with mignardises, also known as petits fours, served on a clay plate. This time, however, the clay is baked and gilded. This is how we establish a link to the past, to the Golden Age of the Rupelstreek, when everybody was after our clay. Reet is the beginning and the end. No pun intended.

SALSIFY - SWEET POTATO ›

ONION

THYME

HIBISCUS

BLOOD SORREL

TRUFFLE CAKE

Finger food

The world of food never ceases to amaze me. One food fad after another. From eating insects, cooking the entire animal 'nose to tail', to leaving food to rot. There are so many trends and hypes, but people still shy away from eating with their hands. Traditionally, your fork is placed on the left with your knife to the right. We are only too happy to use these tools to shovel in any type of food, not realising that by doing so, we create a distance between the food and the eater.

Never forget, hands are the perfect instruments to pick meat off the bone or to remove fish bones. Your fingers cannot taste but they can definitely feel; a sensation that adds value to the entire process of tasting. If you grab something with your hands, you get an initial 'finger feel' of what it will taste like in your mouth.

After all, the saying 'it's so good, I could eat my fingers' did not come from nowhere...

'Take your pick from what the world has to offer, but go local where you can.'

Antwerp as a global port

BART: I don't limit myself to local produce. That is mainly due to our location, but also because we can choose from such a wide range of products. Belgium is a logistics centre and it is no problem whatsoever to lay your hands on day-fresh produce from anywhere in Europe and even Asia. Especially when you bear in mind that the port of Antwerp is only a few miles away from Pastorale. Belgium is a culinary playground and it would be a real shame if I did not play it to the full. We are working with produce from all around the world and this filters through to the plate. You get the local 'feel' but you can taste the world.
Ha. I'll have you know that at home I have a large herb garden. I still live in the farmhouse that is owned by my parents and I grow my own vegetables like I used to do: potatoes, carrots, onions... At the moment I am putting a lot of time and effort into my herb garden. After all, herbs lend a lot of flavour to a recipe.

The Cube by Electrolux 2012

Electronica meets architecture meets haute cuisine.

A pop-up project that fits Bart to a tee. On top of the triumphal arch at the Parc du Cinquantenaire in Brussels, everyone was invited to enjoy gastronomy at the highest level. When The Cube was in residence, two star chefs were taking turns, each with his own unique style and identity. Your meal would be prepared by either Sang-Hoon Degeimbre of L'air du temps, or else Bart would be in charge. In the Cube, with the look and feel of a large electronic appliance, a large table was installed. A table that invited people to talk and to share. Also a table that was perfectly attuned to the philosophy of Pastorale. Large wooden boards, 2.5 metres tall and covered with herbs, in the various shades of Brussels By Night, were mounted on the walls of The Cube. Special bowls with a honeycomb structure, just like the design of The Cube, were developed in Val Saint Lambert to bring the entire event in line with the identity of Pastorale. But above all, serving dessert turned into a truly unforgettable moment. People had to get up and were handed an iPad before taking a few steps back. A carpet made of silicon was rolled out and dessert was served on that. This made for a fascinating spectacle in itself. However, it got better. The roll-out was perfectly synchronised with what was happening on the iPad. The screen displayed the very same dessert that was served on the silicon mat, with one difference: the silicon mat now displayed a naked woman. These images, bizarre and quite provocative, went viral in a world that at that time, was not really cut out for virals yet.

THE CUBE

‘Primeur’ (early spring) vegetables

Ask Bart about his favourite food and he will unashamedly respond with ‘peas’. Those very first, sweet, peas that have just sprung from their shells. As a toddler they were his favourite food and, up to this day, they make his taste buds tingle. Peas even make him feel weak at the knees. He loves the taste and also how they are the harbingers of spring.

Bart’s beloved peas are not the only ones. Asparagus, truffles, Brussels sprouts, young cauliflower from Mechelen (Malines). All of these herald a particular month or season of the year. Also, all of these are vegetables eagerly awaited by chefs at the start of each season as they provide a fresh taste sensation. Every single year.

MONKFISH - GREEN ASPARAGUS

TURBOT - ASPARAGUS 'WERCHTER' - SALTY PLANTS - NEW POTATO

Mushroom taco

This taco, made with chickpea flour and mushrooms, is remarkable in itself, but what really makes it special is the presentation. This taco is presented on a plate shaped like a large mushroom to establish the link with the dish and to remain close to the product.
It took much time and effort to bring these mushrooms to Pastorale. Strolling around a village market in France, Bart's interior architect Martijn Dedecker came across an elderly couple who produced organic shapes using a special type of clay. Martijn's spotted the mushrooms. He sent Bart a picture straight away and Bart was so keen that, before long, he made his way to the very same market. He tried to convince the old couple to produce more of their mushrooms for his restaurant. After all, he needed fifty of them. Two problems immediately became apparent. The first stumbling block was the technique used to make the mushrooms. The clay was fired using a specific technique from Japan called 'Raku', which meant that there was a large margin of error. Only one in four mushrooms left the oven in a usable state. Which meant that they needed to produce not fifty, but two hundred mushrooms. The second issue was that the elderly husband needed to go into hospital quite urgently. Nevertheless, they were 100% certain that they wanted to take on this order. They invited Bart to their home to discuss the details. A hospital bed for the husband had already been installed. Bart was given one of the best welcomes he'd ever had, but the coffee ranked amongst the worst ever. The husband and wife team pulled out all the stops to complete the order. Bart collected his mushrooms only two days late.

TACO - MUSHROOMS - GARLIC - OLIVE - GIROLLE ›

PIGEON - SUNROOT - PURPLE KALE - YOGHURT - SEEDS

WHITE CABBAGE

Vegetables for dessert

You don't usually make a dessert with vegetables. Nevertheless, some veg has a high sugar content and can taste lovely as part of a sweet course. At Pastorale we have perfected the fine art of converting the sugars from the vegetables into scrumptious puddings. What's more, we like to add a few surprises and bend the rules of logic whenever we can.

TOPINAMBUR - ORANGE - ALMASSORA PEANUT - JIVARA MILK CHOCOLATE >

CARROT CAKE

KUMQUAT

SHISO ICE CREAM

KIMCHI

PEAR 'DOUBLE FLIP FROM THE GARDEN'

CHERVIL ROOT

CARAMEL

PEBBLES - ROSEMARY CAKE - VERBENA - CHOCOLATE

'Your face changes as soon as you start to cook'

BART: That must be one of the best compliments I have ever received. Because it's true. It doesn't matter what I am cooking. Whether I am grilling a rib-eye steak or making a sandwich, there is always a smile on my face and I will always make sure that it is cooked to perfection and presented in the nicest possible way. It may look like a lot of effort, but to me it comes naturally. I really love the products I work with. We could be talking about ordinary food. Take a mackerel or shad fish. No-one at my level uses that type of fish. But if a piece of fish like that, perfectly filleted and deboned, arrives on your plate with the right accompaniments, all of a sudden it is no longer ordinary or vulgar, just pure enjoyment. This is something I feel is very important. That respect, almost veneration of a product, is what Japanese cuisine has taught me.

'My passion for meat'
Clara Bella

BART: In 2009 I started to take an interest in maturing beef. I was looking for the best techniques and La Table du Boucher in Mons was happy to share their know-how.

One day, their chef organised a contest: who could produce the best cut of mature beef?
I decided to use Holstein beef, a breed that is known for its milk rather than its meat. No-one was more surprised than me when my modest cut won the award. It was even more surprising as my Holstein was rated above cuts made from Kobe, Wagyu or Black Agnus, breeds that are more expensive and are also thought to be of higher quality. Not only when it comes to taste, but also when you look at the whole story. A milk cow is a dual purpose cow. A cow that is bred for its milk, not necessarily for the taste of its meat. An animal like that can be milked for seven to eight years and has a great life before its final journey to the abattoir. You could say that really, we are looking at top quality meat.
The competition was reported in several newspapers and magazines and also landed on the desk of an abattoir in the Netherlands. Their name was Gosschalk and they agreed with me that it wasn't a bad idea to mature so-called inferior meat from a milk cow to add flavour to it and increase its value. One fine day I received a phone call from Gosschalk. Their product was ready. It had matured. I was bowled over by their response. The fact that these people were brave

enough to invite me to taste their matured beef… that will stick in my memory. In the end, not only did this lead to a beautiful friendship, but it was also the start of a business partnership. I was to become the exclusive distributor for Gosschalk in Belgium and the rest of the world, excluding the Netherlands. Not in their own back yard. Oh well, that's the Dutch for you *(said with a wink)*.
One thing led to another. We developed products together. Designed unique machines for specific preparations. We investigated the industrial properties of a carpaccio and back-tracked. People usually try to find a way to mechanise certain trades. We were looking to introduce craft elements to carpaccio that had already been produced on an industrial scale. I'm happy to say that yes, we managed it. In industry, nitrites or other additives are generally used to prolong the storage period of the meat or to prevent discoloration. However, we switched to natural oils that produce nitrite in a natural way. We wanted to use as few additives as possible, ideally to transfer the healthy philosophy of Pastorale to Gosschalk's meat processing business. Not always the easiest thing in the world, but once you have something specific in mind, you have to be consistent.
It just goes to show: much can change in ten years. From picking up knowledge from La Table du Boucher to winning awards for my own, well-matured beef to supplying meat to that very same restaurant. I do hope that the chef doesn't regret helping me out *(laughs)*.

A recipe for perfect beef

To mature beef also means to tenderize it. Maturing processes break down acids, remove juices and make the meat firmer. Maturing allows a piece of meat to acquire a unique identity. That's why it is a rewarding technique to apply.

There are a few golden rules if you want to cook your beef to perfection.

- Use a thick-bottomed frying pan and heat to a high temperature. This is to prevent the pan from cooling down quickly when you add the beef.
- Allow the beef to reach room temperature, this is how it remains tender when frying and doesn't become tough.
- Carefully pat the beef dry before seasoning it, and always add pepper and salt before frying. The beef should then go into the frying pan straight away, otherwise the salt will draw out the juices from the beef.
- Add as little fat as possible to the frying pan. Goose fat is great for frying. This type of fat is heat resistant and gives a lovely crust.
- Don't keep turning over your beef. Fry each side for a minimum of 2-4 minutes to provide a lovely crust and to make sure it cooked the way you like it. The exact number of minutes depends on the thickness of the beef and how you would like it done.
- Never pierce your beef with a fork. Use a spoon or even tongs to turn it over. This avoids juices escaping from the beef.
- Beef should always rest before it is served. It should spend as much time resting as it did cooking, preferably on a pre-heated plate on the grill.

  This gives all of the juices the opportunity to retract into the entire joint of beef.
- Before serving, put the beef back in the frying pan, add a dab of butter and brown on all sides.

MAX GOSSCHALK: Bart came onto our radar in 2013, after we read in the press that he had turned a Holstein cow into a lovely cut of mature beef. As a business, we have much to be proud of but, when it came to product development, we knew we had a lot to learn. We really needed to catch up with the competition. Bart was perfectly placed to help us.

It soon became clear to us that we wanted to use Bart's services. The greatest thing about Bart is that he can improve products. In every area. Yes, he will select top cuts of beef and find out how best to mature them to achieve the very best taste. His focus is also very much on healthy food. His aim is to reduce the use of preserving agents wherever possible and, at the end of the day, he wants his customers to find an honest product on their plate.

Sometimes, we have to put the brakes on and tell Bart that "Hey, for this particular market, this product is more than good enough." Don't forget that Bart tends to set the bar so high for himself that those around him just have to jump that little bit higher. We do have our clashes and disagreements. But they only flow from our shared attitude: we want to create the best product we possibly can. And, from these clashes, the outcome is always positive.

Also, what I have always found surprising about Bart is how easy he finds it to fire people up. He gets things done. He can be quite compelling, forceful but never less than friendly. I recall that we once used a printer who needed one-and-a-

half weeks to print new labels. So we knew that we had to give him plenty of notice.
Then Bart came onto the scene. If he has a particular idea, he wants it to be ready the very next day. Our printer had to sink or swim. Lo and behold, it was suddenly fine to deliver all of the labels the very next day. No problems, no faffing around and everybody was still happy. Isn't that what they call people management? *(laughs)*

If you ask me which project I am most proud of, I don't really know which one to pick. There are so many, and if I am honest, I think the best is still to come. I'm sure that Bart would agree with me. Our story hasn't finished yet.
I don't think that we have seen the last of Bart. Fortunately!

The contract negotiations with Bart will forever be engraved on my memory. To the best of my recollection, it took about three months to sort it all out, before we had crossed the i's and dotted all of the t's. We discussed every single tiny detail. Often they were removed from the contract and then re-inserted. But, having survived three months of nit-picking, when every minute detail was straightened out, we reached an agreement that we could both live with.
That particular contract was then safely locked into a drawer, never to appear again. Look, the relationship between Bart and me is based on confidence and is not written in black and white. This is why we work so well together to create lovely stuff.

CALF'S HEART, MATURED FOR 60 DAYS
CHERVIL ROOT - LYCHEE - BURRATA
FERMENTED TOMATILLO

Calf's heart

BART: I will never stop my quest for unique people with unique products. I know a man in Switzerland who sells calves' hearts. These hearts are matured for forty days and all the veins have been removed. This is done with a very specific technique and, as far as I know, he is the only one who still knows how to do it. These hearts costs sixty euros per kilo and there are only sixty available around the globe. I tried everything in my power to lay my hands on forty. I want to provoke people but, at the same time, I would like to surprise them and give them new worlds to discover. Unique products could be a way of doing that. And if you then get the opportunity to conjure up a calf's heart on the plate, you must grab it with both hands.

SWEETBREAD COOKED IN WAGYU GREASE

DILL

HORSERADISH

RICOTTA DI BUFFALA

SWEETBREAD - COOKED IN WAGYU GREASE - DILL - HORSERADISH - RICOTTA DI BUFFALA

Love of the Oosterschelde

BART: I got to know the Oosterschelde river (Eastern Scheldt in Dutch) only because someone happened to take me there. I was familiar with the produce of the area, but I did not know the location itself. I think that that was the moment I fell in love with that specific place. The products from the waters of the Oosterschelde taste so amazingly pure. Wild eel, garfish I was able to catch myself, fishing for blue crayfish... Really, once you have sampled these, you realise that you don't have to venture too far afield to find good produce.

OOSTERSCHELDE LOBSTER - GENTLY SMOKED - LETTUCE - FLOWERS - PEACH - PINE CONE

Techniques in practice

BONDING

With fish, there are three different types of protein bonding. These different bonds occur at three distinct temperature levels. It may differ slightly depending on the type of fish, but in general you could say that these bonds are formed around 48 °C, at 60 °C and between 80 and 90 °C. Most of the taste experience comes from the first stage of protein bonding. Visually speaking, the fish still looks raw. The second stage of bonding results in a true gem of a dish. The fish is cooked to perfection and people find it suitable for consumption. The third stage of bonding produces tertiary flavours that are no longer pure and refreshing. It is therefore very important to find the perfect cooking temperature.

IMPREGNATING

Most animal and vegetable products have a well-determined structure with a well-known porosity. This helps you to create a sponge effect. As part of the [sous vide] cooking process, the air contained in the product will expand and disappear. When the pressure is brought back to normal, the product will instantly absorb its own cooking juices. There is no longer any need to marinate your ingredients for days on end. You can do it quickly and efficiently. The seasoning (sugar, salt or stock) enters into the core of the product instead of remaining on the surface. What's more, this process does not affect the texture of the ingredients. Instead, they are beautifully preserved without drying out or turning to mush.

LECITHIN

Lecithin is a substance that is used as an emulsifying agent. An emulsifier is a substance that is added to a product containing two ingredients that would not usually mix, to ensure a suitable blend.
Lecithin can also be used to froth up a sauce, or to pump air into your meringues.

COD - COOKED IN SAGE OIL ›

SARDINE - EGGPLANT - CAPUCHIN

MACKEREL MATURED IN SOY FOR 3 DAYS - BARBECUE - RHUBARB - CELERY

ZEALANDISH OYSTER - BARBECUE - DASHI - RADISH - CHARRED TOMATO

32

Jacob Jan Boerma

Jacob Jan is the owner and head chef of De Leest in Vaassen, in the Veluwe region of the Netherlands. He runs the business with his partner Kim Veldman, who is the hostess at this fantastic restaurant. The cuisine offered by Jacob Jan is based on nature, uses organic ingredients and is rooted in French traditional cuisine with a modern twist.

JACOB JAN BOERMAN: When I was a lad I realised quite quickly that the Belgian culinary landscape of 20 years ago was far more interesting than that in the Netherlands. My first job was in Belgium, with Roger Souvereyns at Scholteshof, a top restaurant in Hasselt. That is where I met Bart.

He made an impression on me from the word go. Do you know why? Because even in those days he was committed to Pastorale in a big way, but he spent his day off working at Scholteshof to increase his knowledge. I remember thinking: what type of idiot would do that? A one-and-a-half our drive on your only day off to stand at the cooker of your own free will? Yes, that idiot was Bart De Pooter. He is a real self-made cook. Everything he can do, everything that has made him into that wildly ambitious chef he is now, he has taught himself. Also, he was never above listening to others. I think that is why he finds it so easy to blend classic cuisine with modern influences.

The more I saw of him, the stronger our relationship became. From time to time I helped out at Pastorale on my day off. After all, in those days I was a free Dutchman in Belgium. I had no ties and was hugely inspired by what Bart was doing. Besides his curiosity, Bart's strongest point is his perfectionism. He carried on and on and on until whatever he had on his mind, was on his plate. Sometimes he was such a perfectionist that he lost sight of the bigger picture. Would you like to know what he learnt from me? To put water on the table and to sell. Bart wasn't really into that type of thing.

What makes us into such an exciting duo? Bart and I are friends but with the added element of competition. We like to think that we bring out the best in one another. It can't be a coincidence that we gained our first and second stars at roughly the same time. It's always been a sort of battle between us. Who will be first to achieve his first star, the second one and then add number three? OK, Bart had been running his own restaurant for a little bit longer than me, but all the same I take my hat off to him. As a young lad he built up everything from scratch. I vividly remember the time – it happened at Bart's home – when I could hear my heart break. The most important woman in Bart's life announced that she was leaving the business. Yes, it was his mother. She was a great help to him in the early years so he could put his restaurant on an even keel. And it really broke my heart to hear her say that she would no longer be able to cope with the workload.

CABBAGE

PLANKTON

AVOCADO

ZEALANDISH MUSSEL

COCKLE

SCALLOP

I saw that this was a very difficult moment for Bart as well. Bart and his Mum simply formed a golden partnership in the kitchen.
Yes, we gained our first star at exactly the same time. I got it for De Leest and Bart for Pastorale. In our quest for more and better, we found one another. We felt we had so much in common that we decided to embark on a road trip. From star restaurant to star restaurant. It may sound decadent, but in those days it was the only way to find out what was happening in the culinary world. Long before the days of Twitter and Instagram, the only thing we could rely on were restaurant reviews in the national press. And so we decided to make our way down there in person to find out what was going on.
There is one thing I will never forget about my restaurant tours with Bart. He never ever stopped ordering. We tended to opt for the set menu, but Bart was ordering more and more dishes. He wanted to taste this, have a bite of that, and why not try another pudding? His hunger was insatiable. I don't mean that he just carried on eating, but Bart was hungry for new and exciting discoveries. His ultimate goal was to learn from every mouthful. If he couldn't figure out how a particular taste combination was achieved, or what made up the texture of a foam, croquant or gel, he summoned the chef straight away and asked him to divulge his secrets.
I think this is a particular characteristic of good chefs. They act like sponges. Each and every high-level chef has a huge box of tricks to choose from. They have stolen all of these tricks with their very own eyes and mastered them through years of practice. Only the very, very best invent their own tricks. I have seen Bart do things that I didn't think were possible. Did you know that Bart purchased kitchen equipment without really knowing what he could do with it? But a new kitchen machine did not stay a secret for long. Bart carried on searching and trying until he knew exactly what he could do with it.
One fine day, Bart wanted to visit a museum in Barcelona, but a day by the pool held more attraction for me. And his daughters felt the same. So Bart set off on his own to contemplate works of art.
After a while, we got bored lounging by the pool. With Bart's girls in tow, I ventured out into the city. I recalled that, on one of our road trips, Bart had said that there was no way that his daughters would ever go into a McDonald's. When I saw a McDrive, I steered the car towards it. Up to today, this remains one of the biggest errors of my entire life. The kids turned hysterical. They pulled at my clothes and my hair and would even have scratched my eyes out if I had not turned the car around. That evening, dining with Bart in a two-star restaurant, I had to explain how I had come by these war wounds. Next to him, his two children were sweetly working on their colouring books. Clearly, their Dad's take on food had been instilled into them from a very early age.
To be honest, after three weeks, I was glad to come home and do my own cooking instead of dining out. I'd had my fill.

PORK BELLY

PICKLED SARDINE

LETTUCE

BUCKWHEAT

GINGER

JALAPEÑO

20 days, 50 restaurants, 580 dishes 2003

BART: If you want to reach the top, you have to sample the top. This is why I desperately wanted to find out what was going on in the world of the stars, no matter how much money or effort it took. In 2002 I kicked off my culinary road trip in the company of my good friend Jacob Jan Boerma, who now wields the sceptre in the kitchen of three-star restaurant De Leest at Vaassen. You could call it a gastronomic journey of discovery. Together we covered 12,000 miles and, in a time span of 20 days, visited 50 restaurants and tasted 580 different dishes.
Our journey began at Arnsbourg in the Alsace. We then drove straight to Switzerland where Marc Veyrat elevated me to culinary heights I'd never experienced before with his molecular techniques. Next on our 'to visit' list was Michel Trama ('drama'), in the depths of France but, not far from Bordeaux. Then it was on to Girona where my children, six and eight at the time, joined our road trip.
We were eating our heart out in Catalonia. From starred restaurants, down the tiniest bars deep in the countryside, to having dinner at people's homes. Catalan food is superb! Until the day where, in a restaurant, they served us with fish that had a stronger smell than all of the fish markets combined. As we were one hundred percent certain that this fish had gone off, we sent it back to the kitchen straight away. Until we looked around us and saw fellow diners tucking into the same fish dinner. It turned out to be bacalao, dried and salted fish. They say that a good chef has to taste everything once. And that is what I did. Only once *(laughs)*.
I did not want to be that type of chef who throws ingredients together willy-nilly. Far from it. First and foremost I wanted to tell stories, bring emotions to the fore and create a philosophy that would fit me, the area where I have my roots and Pastorale as a whole. A philosophy is not plucked out of thin air. I needed some time to reflect on my own take on things, but I had to make a start somewhere.
The parting shot was given at Girona, with Barcelona hot on its heels. And then, with Barcelona as our base, we explored the mountains. We had the very best experience of our whole culinary road trip at El Celler de Can Roca, owned by the three Balaguer brothers: Roca, Espaisucre and Oriol. They are now, as they were then, amongst the best patissiers in the world. A veritable monument to patisserie.
We planned to make Vichy our final stop. At least, those were our intentions. The food at Vichy disappointed us to such an extent that we decided to put our foot down on the pedal and drive on, at some speed, to Paris. Where we dined at La Table: Joël Robuchon's Paris establishment. And this is how our journey ended on a positive note. And with a few excess pounds.

AXURIA LAMB

BROCCOLI SHOOTS

MEXICAN MOLE

MINT

MIZUNA CHOCOLATE

Ferran Adrià 2002
Encounters

BART: This road trip was an important culinary lesson in life. But, a few months beforehand, something happened that knocked me for six. I received an invitation from journalist and author Jean-Pierre Gabriël to dine with him and Daniël Ost, resident florist at Pastorale, at El Bulli and El Celler de Can Roca. Both restaurants made a huge impression on me, but it was El Bulli that, despite my young age, made me feel old. Out of the 26 dishes I sampled there, there were only two that I could 'get' and felt I would be able to replicate. The other 24 were entirely in the realm of the unknown. The two dishes I felt I would be able to prepare were the ones closest to classic cuisine, the style of cooking I had mastered and was familiar with. It turned into an enthralling but also frustrating evening. Suddenly, I realised that at the age of 34 I had been shaped by the older generation of chefs and that there was an entirely new world of gastronomy for me to discover. It was one of those seminal events, moments that only happen three or four times in your entire life. I was quite despondent for a while. Two options were open to me: either I accepted my current abilities as a chef and that would be enough for me. Or else, I would have to go and find myself. To set myself a challenge.

Evolution - technique 2005

La Cocina al Vacio – Sous-Vide Cuisine

BART: Roca had written a book: *La Cocina al Vacio – Sous-Vide Cuisine.* The book was written entirely in Spanish, but I knew that it was a treasure trove of information. In Belgium I had it translated into Dutch before I flew back to Spain. Not only to hand over the Dutch version of the book, but also to spend a week working with Roca and to 'steal with my eyes'. As a thank-you for all my efforts I was presented with a Röner, a hot water bath with a constant temperature [used in sous-vide cuisine].

This book and my various encounters with Catalan cuisine led me to experiment more and more in my own kitchen. I had already taken a few small steps to shake up some of my recipes and the way things were done in the kitchen, but I felt more was needed. What I really wanted was a never-experienced tornado; a complete break with the old way of doing things that would pave the way towards a new culinary landscape. I realised I could not do this on my own. And so I did what every chef should do: employ people who are better than him in a certain area. That can be frustrating but also makes for a great learning experience. At one point, people from sixteen different nationalities were cooking in my kitchen. A top team. Everyone stole each other's ideas. And so did I, to my heart's content.

10-YEAR-OLD APPLE - PEAR - CANDIED ›

Singapore 2007

BART: As part of a four-strong team I travelled to Singapore as a guest chef at the World Gourmet Summit festival. With a healthy dose of nerves, an even bigger helping of enthusiasm, but also with plenty of trepidation.
I was completely new to this type of festival. Only one Belgian chef had gone before me: Sang-Hoon Degeimbre of L'air du temps. Our career paths through the kitchen ran more or less in parallel; our friendship was sparked outside of it. We went to Noma together, tried to beat each other at paintball, threw a party for the staff and put each other's gardens in peril by hosting a barbecue.
It didn't come as too much as a surprise when San asked the good people of the Stamford Swissôtel, the best-rated hotel in town, to invite me to take part in their festival.

SANG-HOON: Bart and I have been friends for several years. When we first met, our relationship was based on mutual respect. We have met quite a few times since and we now enjoy a genuine, warm friendship. Partly based on our shared love of food, but playing paintball together and organising staff parties helped us to establish an even deeper bond.
Bart is always keen to explore. With his innate curiosity, almost child-like in nature, he wants to learn all there is to know about new techniques and flavours and what's more, store it in his memory bank. And thanks to this formidable memory bank, built up over the years, he can produce his modern cuisine. A style of cooking that is not only focused on taste. Surprise or provocation come into it as well. Also, throughout Bart's cuisine we observe his love of art and aesthetic appreciation. This book is only the next step in perpetuating his talent. There's much more to come for Bart.

BART: Singapore remains an unforgettable chapter in my life. From the church tower in Reet to the skyscrapers of Singapore. I am quite tall and broad, but over there I had moments where I felt really tiny. This city – so full of life, that cultural mix, six million people in all... I experienced no end of jaw-dropping moments. I was almost overwhelmed by the size, the cleanliness and the general air of 'organisedness' of this city. Even more, the street food available on literally every corner made a big impression on me.
I clearly remember that one evening, I was passing a stall that was selling roast pig. I purchased a bag of pork crackling and merrily went on my way to the metro station to get back to my hotel. On the platform, I opened the bag, almost salivating at the prospect of enjoying this delicacy. I picked out a piece of crackling and within two seconds I was surrounded by the local police. No bones about it: eating when you're waiting for a train is simply not done. I still had one piece of crackling left, which I wanted to stuff into my mouth, but I didn't even manage that. And this concludes my experience of how clean, law-abiding and tidy Singapore really is.
Or can be. This is in stark contrast with the street food stalls dotted around the city. In fact, the dif-

ference could not be greater. Frogs and chickens are slaughtered in plain view. Right there, on the pavement. In the world of street food, the rules of hygiene don't seem to apply in the same way.

This is what my day in Singapore would look like. At eight o'clock in the morning, the General Manager would magically transform my breakfast table into an office desk. We would then be in meetings until about midnight. And then, from midnight until three in the morning, everyone would just be outside. Twenty degrees Celcius, one large table and two dozen plastic plates heaped with food to be passed along and shared. A journey of discovery for all of the taste buds, but also a major source of inspiration: steamed vegetables, a bouillon of sour plums... It was great. It was just truly wonderful. So pure, so free of any conventions. We laughed and forged friendships that would last a lifetime. Every night turned into a party.

Yes, we built some great memories and lived experiences that would last us a lifetime, but this was not a jolly. We had come over here to work, after all. The main aim of the trip was to introduce Pastorale and therefore we gave much thought as to who would be part of the team. In the end, four of us made the journey which meant that we could really put ourselves on the map over there. When we landed in Singapore, our local branch had an occupation rate of only thirty per cent. After three days, this went up to one hundred percent. And after ten days, the teller reached three hundred percent. We were only able to achieve this thanks to a strong concept, great marketing and a generous helping of luck.

And this is where luck came into it: on my third day in Singapore, I was invited for a chat on breakfast television. I wanted to use my creative side and sense of humour to show my love of this city. On live TV I created a dish that visually resembled the city of Singapore, as viewed from the window of my kitchen. Green on the outside and white in the centre, to symbolise the skyscrapers. The entire dish was made of nuts. And I called it: 'only 3 days in Singapore and already nuts about it'. This one single sentence was copied by all of the newspapers and other media: *'CRAZY BELGIAN CHEF IN THE STAMFORD SWISSOTEL'.* That night, we had no problems filling the restaurant. And over the following days, the telephone did not stop ringing. One single sentence and one single dish. That is all it took to conquer many Singaporean hearts. I had never experienced anything like it. And, it was the first time that I got even close to star status. I must admit that it gave me a huge ego boost. Fortunately, I was mature enough to keep both feet on the ground and just carry on with my job. Nevertheless, I have to admit that it took me some time to settle back into my life in Belgium. On one particular occasion, when I was busy cooking, I asked my wife to pass me a particular ingredient. She said no, absolutely not; she was busy doing her own thing. And what I said, up to this day, is still clear in my mind: 'I am only asking you for a very small favour. And I am asking you very kindly.' In Singapore my single concern was my own wellbeing. All it took was for me to click my fingers to get whatever I wanted. I only had to think of a product and someone would be standing right next to me handing it to me on a plate. Yes, I needed some time to adjust when I came back *(laughs).*

MY TABLE AT 2 O CLOCK AM

Hong Kong 2008

BART: If you manage to fill an entire restaurant within only a few days and increase the occupation rate from thirty percent to three hundred percent, it doesn't go unnoticed. It appeared that the Mira Group kept a close watch on me. The face behind this company, a businessman who is sometimes known as the Asian Warren Buffett, invited me to participate in a hotel project in Hong Kong.

During my stay in Singapore I'd already noticed that the luxury segment of the hospitality industry has a very pro-active approach to the comfort of its guests. I found that in Hong Kong, things are much the same. All the way from a personal butler, who was ready to be our guide through the city, down to linking up your smartphone to a purpose-built system that allowed your taxi driver to know your exact destination in one single glance.

Unlike Singapore, home to a multitude of expats and subject to major Western influences, Hong Kong felt really Chinese. This showed up in the way people were living and eating. In Hong Kong you still find all of those authentic, Chinese cuisines. Yes, I am using the plural for a good reason, as there are so many different cuisines. Due to the size of the country and the resulting presence of many different people each with their own cultures, plus all the different climates and local food sources, you cannot talk about one single 'cuisine'. Which, for me, made China into a journey of culinary discovery.

Oh well, we did not spend the whole day exploring. After all, we made this trip with the purpose of opening a restaurant in Hong Kong that would be grounded in the Pastorale philosophy. We worked our socks off, over a three-month period, to try and create this story. Unfortunately, it turned out to be only half a story. Despite all of the time and effort I had spent on coming up with ideas and the actual preparation time, a crisis did break out. As I had signed quite a lucrative contract, I was not willing to engage in endless rounds of re-negotiation and thus my contract was withdrawn from one day to the next. Hong Kong for me was a beautiful experience, but without a happy ending, really, only half a happy ending. I don't look upon it as a failed project. Rather, the circumstances were unfortunate and the timing could have been much better. There is nothing we could have done to make this venture a success. From my point of view, I learned a lot during my stay, both about myself and about life in general.

Tokyo 2012

BART: If I had to pick one city in Asia where I would be happy to live, it would be Tokyo. As Japan is an island, its culture is still very authentic and pure. Also, due to its length, you can experience four different seasons within one country if you travel from North to South. In Japan, there is so much to explore and to discover that, so far, it feels like I have spent three hundred years of my life over there. What appealed to me straight away about Japan were its supermarkets, the diversity and purity of the products and the patience and honesty of its people. Plus, I was impressed with the country's natural landscape.
To start off with, I was invited to the cities of Tokyo and Osaka to draw up a fine dining concept for the Japanese market. It didn't stop there: I also came up with the idea for a beer cuisine with potato-based sushi and carried out an analysis of the importance of hamburgers in the gastronomic landscape of Japan. And, I was also there to promote Belgian waffles. My arrival at the airport will forever stay in my mind. I landed with three suitcases stuffed to the brim with everything I needed to make my waffles. Needless to say, the Customs people took me to one side. I may be a chef, but to arrive in Japan, completely unannounced, with bags full of food is not (yet) one of my privileges.

With fear in my heart and a sunny smile on my face, I opened my suitcases. I explained to the friendly lady employed by Customs that all of this was for home consumption and for use at parties. Whereupon she stated: 'Congratulations Sir, you know what your answers should be.'
After which they searched every square centimetre of my suitcases, opened every single – carefully wrapped – present and grilled me on every single ingredient. At the end of the day, I had nothing to hide and so I was allowed to leave. But not before they took a few selfies with me.

So how did I get to know so many people in Japan? I finished work at 15:00 and then, from 16:00 onwards, started to cook for them in my own home, or wherever I was at the time. When I say 'them', I mean that I invited ten people who were asked to bring one guest each. Bear in mind that in Japanese culture you are responsible for your 'plus one'.

Every duo would contribute a dish of their own. This allowed me to sample at least ten different dishes every single evening. My 'soirees' became the stuff of legend, or should I say notoriety? Invariably we kicked off our evenings with a Corona, followed by a home-made Sangria. A Riesling would be great with dinner and after the meal, it was time to bring out the saké. At the start of proceedings, not many words were said. When the night drew to a close, everybody was fluent in English. And I found that my Japanese had come along in leaps and bounds. At least, that's what it felt like at the time. Oh well, these sessions allowed me to get to meet a great variety of people in a very short space of time. I also established a network that has served me well up to this day and I still keep in touch with some of these friends.

‹ VIEW FROM MY ROOM

Sosei Kazuki is Bart's main business partner in Japan. Both of Sosei's parents were fashion journalists who introduced the Armani brand to Japan and, going East to West, exported some of the main Japanese fashion names into Europe. Sosei now works on Bart's behalf to make the two worlds meet once again, although the world we are now referring to is the one of food. He is far more than 'just' a business partner. Sosei is Bart's confidant in Japan as well as a loyal friend.

SOSEI KAZUKI: Life is full of chance encounters. Some of these meetings remain superficial and others take on a great intensity within only a short period of time. Without a shade of a doubt, Bart fell into the latter category. I was working on a large project in Berlin when the COO took me out on a trip and met Bart's wife, Stefanie Hering. She is a talented ceramic artist and I became her distributor for the Japanese market. When, one fine day, my team and I had to design an entire building, I was in sudden need of Stefanie's services. The new building was located almost straight across from the Royal Imperial Palace, the main residence of the Emperor of Japan. This in itself didn't particularly faze me, but my boss insisted that this flagship project could absolutely not be allowed to fail. And thus he was looking for inspiration to add some cachet to the restaurant on the ground floor. Straight after the meeting I got on the phone to my favourite potter.

Stefanie introduced me to Bart. From the off, we had a great connection. Bart and I took the same view: that opening up a restaurant in the first building, would be a step-up to doing further business in Japan.

I always felt that Bart had a dual motive. On the one hand, he was a frequent business visitor to Japan. On the other hand, I have always felt that Japan has a special place in his heart. That he doesn't only visit the country for business, but also for his own enjoyment. I showed him around all of the spots that I felt would appeal to him: small, quirky restaurants; a ski resort, supermarkets with a gigantic product range, food exhibitions...

We were not only in search of great restaurant projects. We were also on a continuous lookout for the very best produce. Products that could add value to Pastorale. In those days, Wagyu beef was becoming increasingly popular in Europe. However, what we wanted to take back to Europe with us was Kobe beef. There often is a confusion between Wagyu and Kobe beef. All Kobe beef is Wagyu, but not every Wagyu steak comes from Kobe. The beef is only called Kobe if it originates from the prefecture of Hyogo (Kobe is its capital) and if the cattle were slaughtered there.

It is far from easy to export and distribute this particular beef. We Japanese are proud of our produce but at the same time, we like to play

our cards close to our chest. However, Bart and I formed a formidable team with some great benefits. I am a Japanese with plenty of experience in the world of import and export. Bart already had ties with Gosschalk, an abattoir in the Netherlands and was thus able to bring a reliable partner to the team. A golden combination, perfectly equipped to bring Kobe beef to the shores of Europe.
Nevertheless, Kobe is not even Bart's main export product. He acted as a consultant for a chain and there was a call for noodles. One fine day we decided to visit Foodex, a large food exhibition with numerous stands showcasing Japan's best produce. All of a sudden he stopped at the smallest booth. They were selling 'somen' noodles with green tea. Behind that little stand, a big story was hidden. It was a store that had been in the same family for three generations and, what's more, supplied practically every two-starred and three-starred businesses in Japan. They don't come more authentic than that. Fortunately, Bart did come across them and became the main importer of these noodles into Europe. This is not only a blessing for them, but also for the families who produce these noodles: no fewer than 20 people depend entirely on his import business.
This year we exported around 14 tonnes of noodles. Next year we will be aiming for 36 tonnes. I am 99% certain that Bart is set to conquer the world with simple noodles *(laughs)*.
Bart has a unique take on being a chef. Star chefs are very focused on their own kitchen and often forget that outside of those four walls, there is an entire world to discover and to open up. Bart is different. He is constantly moving his own boundaries to bring the best that the world has to offer into his kitchen. And he is not just doing that because he enjoys it: he has a sincere desire to share those things with his guests. I admire that. I don't need to tell you that Bart is also a brilliant cook. But, he has an instinct for business that you don't often come across. And in this world, with all its restrictions, rules and regulations that restaurants have to live by, is something you can't do without.

BART: I was invited to attend a cookery demo: how to carve a squid. In Japan, carving techniques are almost out of this world. It takes years of experience and much practice to master them completely. During the demo, a Spaniard who was quite full of himself stood up and stated, with a fair bit of arrogance, that he could do that just as well. The Japanese chef, very humbly, presented the knife to the Spaniard with both hands accompanied by the words *'Please sir, do it'*. From a visual point of view, the pieces looked almost identical. But they were then put to the taste. The piece of squid cut by the Japanese chef melted on the tongue; the Spaniard's efforts had a rubbery structure and were only fit for the bin. The only difference was the cutting technique, involving cutting every fibre, horizontally or vertically, for up to a hundred times. The best demonstration of respect for the product that I have ever seen.

Japan taught me humility. An attitude that has taken me far. Especially in combination with my no-nonsense approach *(laughs)*.

This story provides me with a seamless transition to Jiro Ono, an eighty-year-old man who has teamed up with his sixty-year-old son to run a sushi restaurant in a decomissioned train station. Jean-Pierre Gabriël, the very same journalist who introduced me to El Bulli, tipped me off that Jiro was a must visit when I next came to Japan. As a Westerner it was well-nigh impossible to get in. Every day, only twelve people were given the opportunity to take a seat at his table. Thanks to Sosei we managed to reserve two. When we had made our way in, we were given fourteen different pieces of sushi to eat. The chef determined the pace of the meal and had given careful consideration to the times between each piece of sushi.

Jiro also taught me how to put a really good sushi together: what the temperature must be at the time of eating, which flavourings to use and how the fish or the meat ought to be carved to avoid any toughness. What struck me the most about the entire meal was that the old man did almost everything by himself. The son was only allowed to cook rice. His father clearly felt that, even at the advanced age of sixty, his son was not yet cut out for the real work.

One night I was invited, together with my legal representative, to a dinner where traditional dress would be worn. In my hotel room I found a choice of two kimonos, each suspended on their own hanger. A tiny but amusing detail: my interpreter and general assistant was Miss Japan 2008. As I had never worn a kimono before, I asked Miss Japan to help. Nothing was too much for her so she came up to my room to make sure that my kimono was draped as it should be and everything was in the right place. Confident that I would make a great impression, I made my way down to the reception area, where I spotted Roel Nieuwdorp, my travelling companion, confidant and legal adviser. Clearly, he had not felt the need for assistance and consequently, his outfit looked a bit crumpled. My chest was swelling with even more pride. Proud as a peacock, I continued my descent of the staircase, only to be met with what I can only describe as looks of utter befuddlement. It still felt like the best entrance I had ever made until... everyone burst out laughing. Now it was my turn to look befuddled. Apparently, I was wearing the kimono in the Japanese women's way. Miss Japan got it wrong. She had tied the kimono in the same way she would dress herself. So, that evening, I was dressed as a woman. Oh well, it was funny in a way and I had a laugh myself. *'This evening I'm a woman'*, is what I said to the group.

The following morning, we were having breakfast once again in traditional attire. I tied up my kimono myself, got it right this time, sat down at the breakfast table and said: *'Today I'm a man'*.

SKREI MATURED FOR 3 DAYS IN MISO - SAKÉ

CABBAGE - FERMENTED GREEN STRAWBERRY - GINGER - SHISO

bartOwaffles
bartOwaffles

BARTO WAFFLES - MARZIPAN

Salt water

If you are in need of salt water, you have two options open to you. The first, and easiest option: take some water and add some salt. Option two: you procure it from where you find the very best salt water in the world, e.g. three hundred metres below the sea level in Japan. At this depth, the sea is immobile and the water will have the highest mineral content.
This water is now reduced to seventy percent and is used to add a salty flavouring to sauces or to make a bouillon, or stock. Why would you boil up salty sea water instead of just using water and sea salt? This particular technique makes for an entirely different flavour. It lengthens the mouth and broadens the tongue. Do you want umami? *This* really is umami.
So what is the price of one litre of this salty sea water? 25 euros per litre.

GILLARDEAU OYSTER - CELERY - PICKLED GOOSEBERRY - GREEN APPLE ›

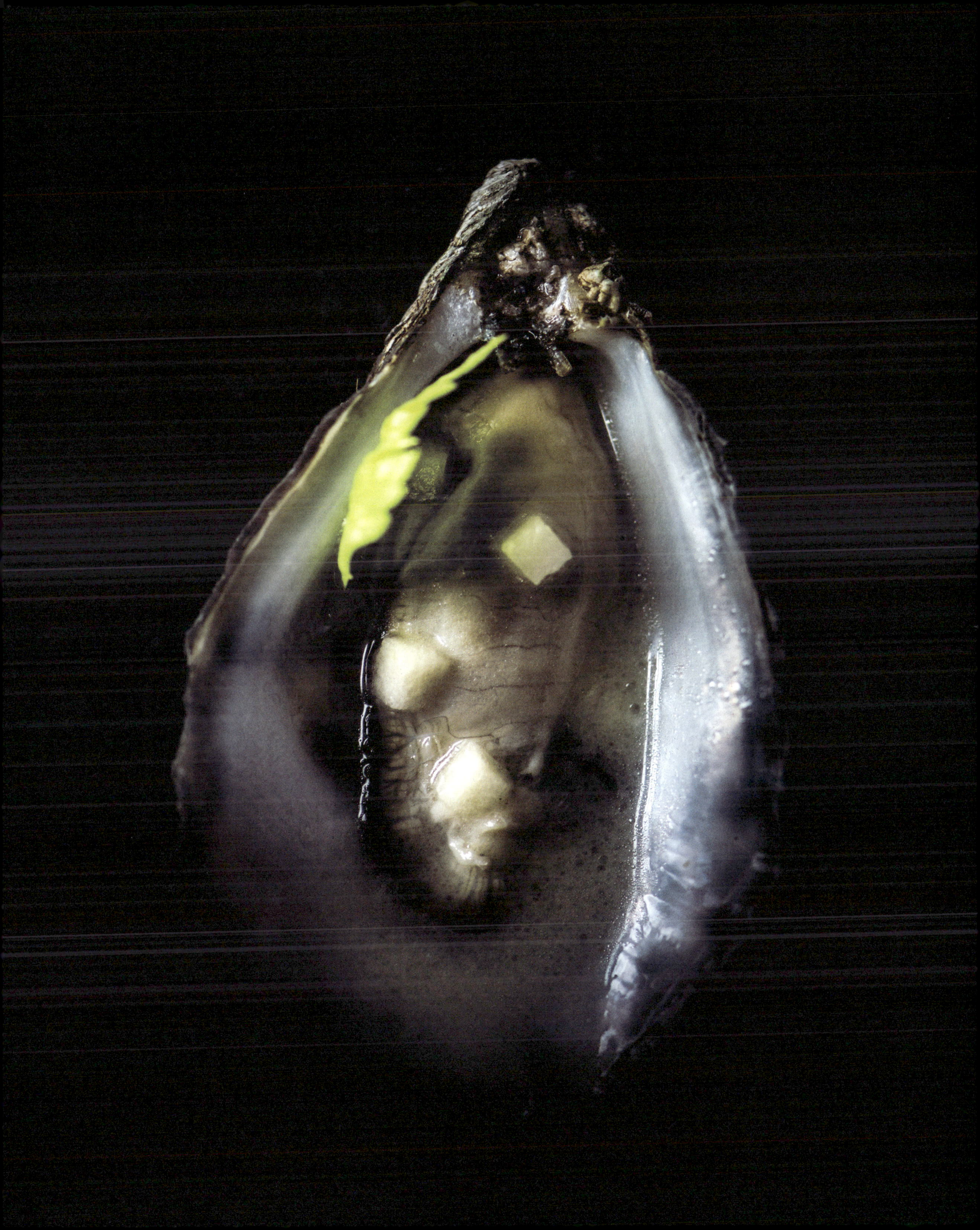

GILLARDEAU OYSTER - BARBECUE - PICKLED GOOSEBERRY - ASHES

Potato sushi

BART: During my stay in Japan I was also asked to come up with a fast food concept that was new to the market. I decided to replace the most common local ingredient with the most common Belgian ingredient: substituting potatoes for rice. Japan has some lovely varieties of potato so I had a few to choose from. Moreover, this would be a great opportunity to translate the Belgian food culture into convenient, ready-to-eat sushi. Yes, I used potatoes, but I finished them off with typical sushi *toppings*. Wagyu, Kobe, glazed eel to name but a few... I have to admit, I had great fun. As the cherry on the cake, or as the Wagyu on the fries if you prefer, our friendly designer, Anouk Van Ranst, created potatoes out of porcelain on which to serve our creations.

POTATO SUSHI - MUSSEL - COCKLE - RED MULLET

POTATO SUSHI - MUSHROOM - SORREL

Beijing 2012

BART: In 2012 I was invited to take part in a culinary competition in Beijing. It really was a strategic jousting game where you were not only asked to serve a tasty meal – every single detail could make a huge amount of difference. The concept of this competition was to prepare six dishes for 26 people in two hours' time. You would be up against another team consisting of four members. That is quite a challenge. But, they upped the ante.

Eighty ingredients were laid out on the table. The teams had to take turns to pick an ingredient. Straight away, my opponent selected the best ingredient from the table. I picked the worst one: intestines filled with sea water and sand. I had absolutely no idea what I could do with them and, just for that reason, I knew that they might come in useful at a later stage. And this is how it carried on until all of the eighty products had been allocated. Just a tiny detail: each team was allowed to 'steal' an ingredient from the other team by substituting it with another. No prizes for guessing what I swapped with my opponent.

So I got rid of these intestines, filled with salt and sea water, early in the game. I really had no idea what I could possibly use them for. And now my opponent had to incorporate them into one of his dishes. He had tried to steal my trump card from under my nose, but ended up with the dud. A contest after my own heart.

The previous day I had already noticed that this culinary competition was primarily strategic in nature. I had explored the lay of the land at earlier duels and it struck me almost instantly that the teams from Asia stood a far larger chance of winning. After all, the jury was from Asia. Thanks to my travels in the East I had become familiar with quite a few different techniques, products and finesses of the Eastern way of cooking. A lot of finger food and small portions. I slightly adjusted my way of cooking to local culture and made sure that everything could be eaten with chopsticks. Needless to say, I always stuck to my own philosophy. As a result, the jury was unable to distinguish between my own dishes and those prepared by my Chinese opponent.

There was nothing to gain but honour. But there was plenty to lose. The losing team had to consume a local delicacy. Ugly food. When we were fighting it out, the booby prize was a bull's penis. I still remember that, just before the contest, I told the lady presenter: 'I've never had a cock in my mouth and I would like to keep it that way.' She blushed and walked away from me.

Oh well, I ended up winning the contest. All well and good. But the curiosity of a chef often wins out over taste. So, I decided to take a bite of the ugly food. So, for a short time, I was 'a kok (pronounced as 'cock') with a penis in his mouth'. Moreover, this was broadcast on live TV to over 120 million viewers.

Beijing is such a large city that even its taxi drivers barely know their way around. At any rate, we reached our destination around 2.5 hours after setting off.

A small woman, very friendly, was waiting for us. Wrapped up in a thick down coat. I guess it was around 8 degrees outside. Indoors as well. She handed me my key and I found my way to my room. Which was freezing cold. The rooms were not heated and there was no oil heater. So, back to Reception. It took a while but, using sign language, I was finally able to explain the problem. Apparently we had timed our arrival wrong: we were two days early. In China you are only allowed to turn your heating on from 1 November. A slice of communism put into practice.

An entirely new culinary world opened up for me. Beijing is still very much a city of culture and tradition. And you can be either for or against, because it does give rise to some ethical questions and objections. This is where I tasted dog and cockroach for the first time. But the typical street food of this city was superb. Peking duck, tuna dumplings, crickets...

I wanted to witness all these goings-on from up close. I was walking past the street food stalls every single day and any further restraint was futile. Plucking up all of my courage, I joined a local beauty at her cosy stall. We cooked together for half an hour so I could learn the tricks of the trade. And impress the local beauty next to me. Although I didn't get anywhere with her, I did sell truckloads of dumplings with dried tuna and tuna sauce.

174 KOBE ROLL - NEW VEGETABLES - AVOCADO

Moscow 2014

BART: I travelled to Moscow on the invitation of the Omnivore organisation who wanted to promote European cuisine in Russia's capital. Moscow was the complete antithesis to Japan in every possible way. Whereas the land of the rising sun offers a gigantic diversity of products, in Russia you have to use the same products all the time. Moreover, their budget was rather more limited. Tuna steaks costing a few thousand euros are unheard of. For a chef who likes to discover new things and likes to keep his options open, this is hard to get to grips with.

In Moscow I learned to prepare *borscht*, a Russian soup based on red beetroot. I also learned various techniques for pickling and salting meat and vegetables. Over there this is done on a far larger scale than here in Belgium. Many people live far from the city and, during the cold winter months, want to have enough food in store to survive. So they will pickle lots of different products and store them in their cellar to use them when needed.

I have been to Moscow three times. Once with the organisation and twice at my own initiative. The second time I also visited Saint-Petersburg and went further into the countryside to seek contact with the locals. I was very curious as to their way of life. This is how I ended up seeing the *dachas*, villas surrounded by very fertile land. These were built especially for army veterans as a thank-you for their support of Russia.

I also browsed the local markets with journalists and television cameras in my wake. One of the journalists asked me if I could find everything that was available in Belgium. Yes, that was indeed the case. I really did see all of the products that I could buy in my own country. However, they were far more expensive. This last comment ended up on the cutting room floor.

The vast majority of the population did not have access to most of these products and had to make do with potatoes from Estonia, beetroot, pork knuckle... Some people are more fortunate and are able to grow extra vegetables in their own garden. In that case, they were really privileged.

I'll have you know that at the time I was there, over seventy percent of produce was imported, a huge percentage.

Rome 2006

BART: We have been collaborating for years with a brand with which I can identify completely: Nespresso. With them, I really discovered coffee. In Switzerland they plunged me into the world of the black, liquid gold. They also gave me the opportunity to create my own coffee, a blend as they call it. Moments such as these are a unique experience for a chef. You are given the chance to work with an ingredient and components with which you are unfamiliar. It is a step into the dark, but it is a chef's favourite thing to expand his boundaries and seek his own enlightenment. This was just the same for me when it came to coffee. They let us start from base zero: select the green beans, roast, determine the bitterness, add acids and so on. We were playing around with percentages, with the various notes in the flavours of the roast beans, with the way they were ground. It was wonderful to get my head around all of those options and be able to use them. And before I knew it, I had blended my own unique coffee. That was great. I thought it was delicious, but I fear that it is not accessible enough for the mass market.

That's when you realise that it is far from easy to blend coffee. Just like I have worked hard for many years to master as many techniques as possible, the master blenders are also real chefs filled with passion. They are handed a large tool kit which they put to good use to make the best coffees.

Total Taste with Nespresso

BART: Yes, I am giving Nespresso a great podium at Pastorale, but they also offered me the opportunity to climb the podium in Rome. This was to introduce the Total Taste concept, the predecessor of the philosophy around biotope. I was looking forward to it so much, but literally everything that could go wrong, did go wrong. It would turn out to be my most difficult presentation ever.

When I arrived in Rome I found that my luggage had been delayed by two hours. To add insult to injury, it had been damaged as well. A taxi sped me, in the manner of Formula 1, to the presentation room but even so, I arrived late on the scene. I was on time for the presentation, but I arrived too late to check out the podium and the equipment. Something that is absolutely key for a speaker.

I made my entrance on the podium and was unable to see the audience. The lights were so bright that it felt like I was talking to a wall. Whereas interaction and contact with the audience are of prime importance to me. To boost my confidence I pulled my already prepared text from my trouser pocket, placed it on the lectern and read it out. It was a story full of emotion and replete with knowledge. I had worked for years to create this story. Instead of presenting it in my own way, I just read out the words. At moments such as these I am an open book. The people in the audience must have felt that something was awry, apart from the contents obviously. I also felt that the client deserved better from me.

Oh well, you learn from your mistakes. From that moment onwards I have never trodden on a podium with a sheet of paper in my trouser pocket. I'd rather spend a quarter of an hour searching for words than losing the spontaneity and the emotion from an impromptu speech.

TOTAL TASTE 2005

In 2005 Bart introduces Total Taste. The first launch of this new concept took place in San Sebastian, 'lo mejor de la gastronomía', with national radio and television in his wake. Later, Belgium, the Flemish Foodies and Pastorale followed. Total Taste is a marketing concept translated into cooking.

The model is comprised of two axes. The vertical axis distinguishes between the human being and the product; on the horizontal axis we see the physical taste on the one hand, the psychological taste on the other. In other words, the model is based on the individual as well as the product, applied to thoughts and visual aspects. This is how we establish the four quadrants: the four tastes that work together to deliver a total experience. Total Taste.

The first port of call is the physical need or habit. The expectation. What do we expect from our food nowadays? Should it be easy to digest, low in fat and sugar, have a high vegetable content and should it be good for you? Grown locally? Or are you mainly concerned about health?

The reverse of the coin is the psychological need. You could define it as the pattern of expectations, the sensory images you build of a food item: aroma, structure, temperature, sound and the overall look. To all of these, Pastorale adds an extra stimulus: childhood memories, irony, surprise, provocation, fun and deception. Just to give you an example of childhood memories. If you think of an apple it comes with a certain pattern of expectations. For example, you would expect this apple to have a sweet fragrance, to have a reddish colour, to crunch when you bite into it and to be sour in taste. At Pastorale we go one step further: we will provide an apple of such high quality, shiny and crunchy to such an extent, that it takes you back to your grandparents' orchard where you used to pick fresh apples as a child. And then there's another surprise in store for you: a tarte tatin that does not look like a tarte tatin but tastes like it.

The psychological aspect of the product is its image. It's about playing around with different elements: the graphic design, the environment, the service, the integration with art, a variety of communication channels and the lay-out of the plate. Take a look at how the service is performed, for example. Preferably, it should surprise and stimulate and come with a clear explanation. The guest must also have information so he or she can draw the maximum enjoyment from the sensory experience and the dish itself.

The final quadrant of the model: the physical qualities of the product and the dish. Here, the starting point is the purity of the food itself, which should be ecologically sustainable and adhere to the strictest of quality standards. Technology and know-how are added into the mix.

In this way the product is approached from different structures: pluralism, symbiosis (which would grow into biotope), minimalism, reconstruction, deconstruction, association and others.

At Pastorale, these four patterns put together, are called 'Total taste'. This has been a constant guideline for us to develop our own biotope.

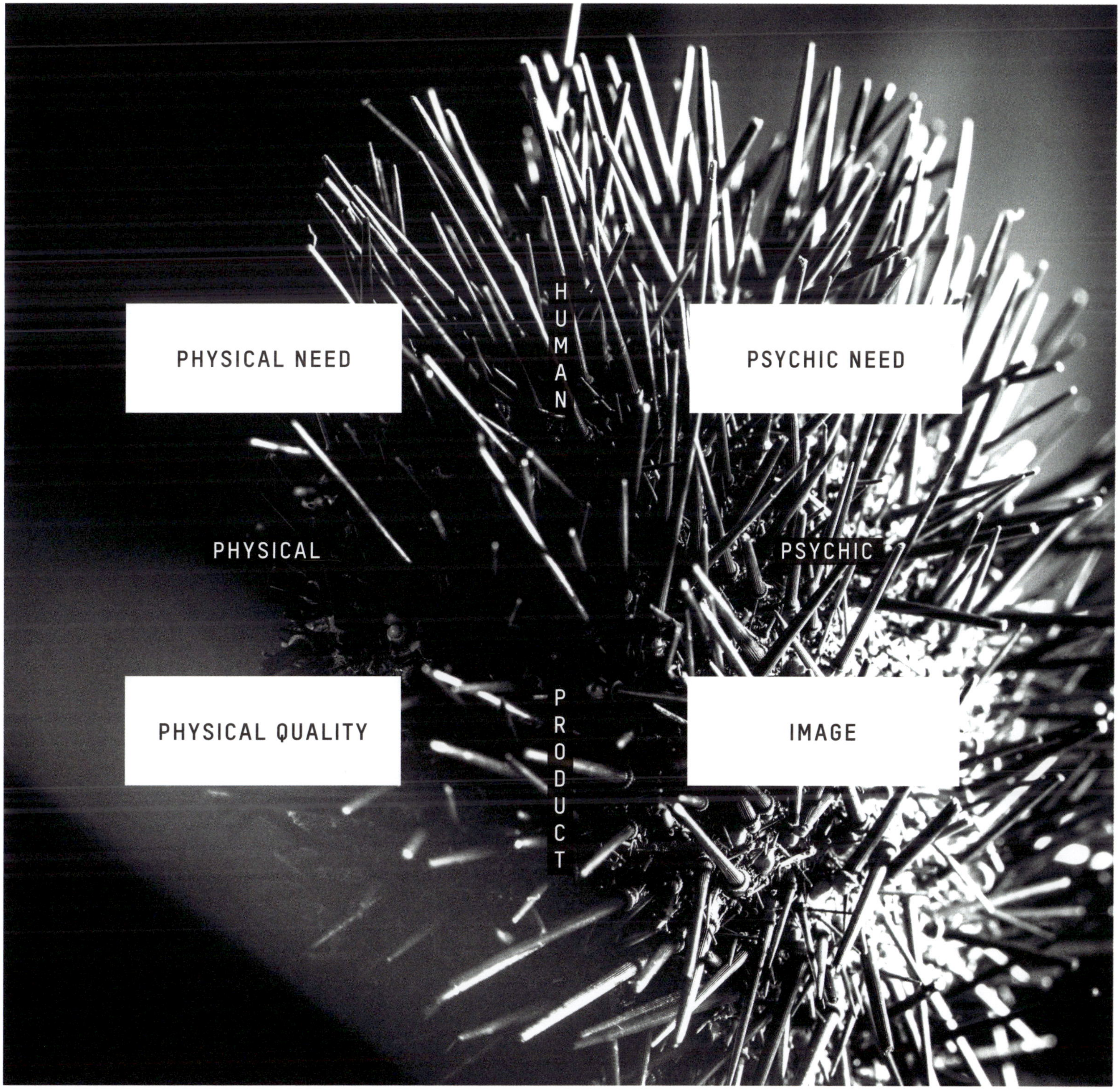
PHYSICAL NEED
HUMAN
PSYCHIC NEED
PHYSICAL
PSYCHIC
PHYSICAL QUALITY
PRODUCT
IMAGE

Helge Kirchberger Photography / Red Bull Hangar-7

Salzburg 2013

In the world of hospitality, the name of Hangar-7 packs a big punch. Dietrich Mateschitz, the founder and manager of Red Bull, was the initiator of this splendid edifice in Salzburg. The ground floor is home to an exquisite display of aeroplanes, helicopters, Formula 1 racing cars and a plethora of other exceptional means of transport. The collection is maintained by a 60-strong team. Press the button in the elevator to take you three floors up and you will find yourself in a restaurant that bears the name of Ikarus. You could say that Ikarus is 'winging it' as its menu changes on a monthly basis, just like its chef. Peter Goossens, Sergio Herman, Jonnie Boer, René Redzepi, Virgilio Martínez... these are just a few big names from the culinary world who were guest chefs at Hangar-7. In November 2013 it was Bart's turn to express his vision on food and dining amongst the aeroplanes, lakes and mountains of Salzburg.

BART: I really enjoyed my brief stint cooking in Salzburg. We were all given plenty of time and space to do our 'prep'. We were allowed to stick to our own philosophy and, what's more, could always rely on the services of a good kitchen team under the capable management of Roland Trettl. In the first week that your menu is served to guests, a tasting is held where you can make some last-minute tweaks.

Salzburg was another great combo of *work hard, play hard.* Once I had fine-tuned my recipes, I was plunged head over heels into the world of Red Bull. One morning in particular, they invited me to enjoy half an hour of aerial acrobatics with the world champion. I was subjected to the most death-defying stunts and that on an empty stomach. Loop-the-loop, corkscrews... you name it, he did it. I was in the front seat with the pilot behind me. The experience went up another gear once I was allowed to take over the controls and execute my own stunts. I performed a few corkscrews and then over the lake at Red Bull's headquarters, upside down. Three metres above the water with the control stick firmly in my grasp. The pilot asked me if I would mind going up just that little bit higher... five metres for example. That did put a smile on my face.

As fate would have it, in the same week I was in Salzburg, Sebastian Vettel won the Formula 1 world championship in Brazil. He was promptly flown back to Salzburg and I was asked to assist with the celebrations, not only in Hangar-7 but in other locations as well. That night we strutted our stuff at a local disco until we were kicked out and I also learnt to drink vodka-Red Bull. That night I proved that the slogan 'Red Bull gives you wings' is 100% true.

IN FOOD WE TRUST
IN FOOD WE TRUST
IN FOOD WE TRUST

Business is pleasure 24 hours in Londen 2003

BART: In the early hours we took the Eurostar to London. The four of us – Jan Bleys and two of my team members, Michiel De Bruyn and Wouter Van Der Vieren – had an audience with Heston Blumenthal. We were looking forward to a fantastic day and an extraordinary experience. Before making our way to Heston's The Fat Duck, we wandered down a little road completely lined with book stores. I was browsing the cookery books and so were my team members; Jan was taking a particular interest in the architectural tomes.

We had such an interesting time of it that we forgot to keep our eye on the clock. We were in grave danger of missing our train to Maidenhead. Close to despair, we waved down a taxi driver: 'Please Sir, we're in a rush. Our train is leaving in ten minutes'. He looked us up and down… 'I will do my best; jump in.' We flew through London at the speed of light, sometimes even using the pavement to overtake the stationary traffic. We felt like actors in a James Bond movie. The bottom line: we made it. We boarded the train with seconds to spare before the doors slammed shut. Just imagine, such a foolish way to lose your table in the restaurant that you'd been looking forward to for such a long time!

Well, I call it a restaurant, but it is more like a laboratory. Very high-tech with so much thought going into it. Our experiences will stay with us forever. There was a lot of focus on sensations and childhood memories. We were served real mind tricks and were constantly wrong-footed. At one point we were served an ice cream, with a lovely pink colour in the middle, covered in dark chocolate. When you bit into it, you got a salmon flavour. That was completely bizarre, but also very tasty.

I was simply blown away by the vision and passion of Heston's way of cooking. It was not my ultimate dining experience, but as a story, it was brilliantly composed.

We had to flush this overwhelming experience out of our system. We did this at Sketch in London, the restaurant of Michelin chef Pierre Gagnaire. Initially we were told that no tables were available, but after a brief introduction, they found some space for us. Fortunately for us, but also for Sketch and their bank balance. We probably ate everything on the menu and tried all of their cocktails at least three times over.

Besides winning a clutch of stars, this venue has also scooped pretty much every architectural award going. Thoroughly deserved. An idiosyncratic interior, crafts on a small scale, high level, never kitsch. To show you what I mean: pots of epoxy paint in various colours were poured down the oak staircase. The effect can only be called enchanting. This place is worth a visit just for its toilets. In some type of mirrored room there are six eggs that serve as toilet areas. Believe me, if you have been indulging in a few cocktails and you set foot into that room… for a moment you have lost all of your bearings. Oh well, after the Heston experience, not much would faze us.

When we made our way back to the hotel, a little worse for wear, it was also almost time to go back home. We managed an hour's kip before boarding the Eurostar, not speaking much and clutching our sore heads. This trip was rather full-on, but it will forever be etched on our memories and also, we expanded our boundaries. Look, I work hard, I want to see and taste everything, but I also want to enjoy it with friends and just let my hair down from time to time. Anyway, we were back in the Pastorale kitchen at 9am. As if nothing had happened.

Paris, the city of light 1993

DUCASSE – **BART:** I will never forget my first time in Paris. I was only a young chef and had been invited to dine at Alain Ducasse. His restaurant was the first three-star establishment where I had ever crossed the threshold. I was 23 years of age and had just started working out the concept of Pastorale. I was consumed by nerves only because I had been invited to enjoy fine food. Can you put yourself in my shoes? I had even practiced my French for this special occasion. I wanted to come prepared and had a few questions ready. What I hoped to gain from this visit was to build on my knowledge and to come away with plenty of fresh inspiration. After so many years, my most vivid memory of the evening is how I opened that door, took in all the different sights and was just about able to say 'bonjour' in a halting voice. 'Goedendag, mijnheer De Pooter', was the first voice that came to my ears. Yes, I was spoken to in Dutch. By people who not only knew my name, they were also aware of who I was and where I came from. It turned out that they did a quick search on the name of every guest, so they could brief reception on how to greet him or her. And so I was assigned the only Dutch-speaking employee, who would stay with me throughout the evening, to introduce me to the world of Ducasse. That just felt so special to me. And this made me realise: the difference really is all in the detail. Oh, and let's not forget the various courses *(said with a wink)*. I remember every single one of them. Even the few more glasses of wine and the bread roll 'for the road' made a lasting impression on me.

GAGNAIRE – **BART:** If I have to choose one chef, the one I would put on a pedestal and I respect the most, I can only say Pierre Gagnaire. His Parisian establishment, Gaya Rive Gauche, is a restaurant where I take great pleasure in dining and that I leave, every single time, inspired and impressed.
Pierre creates the most wonderful taste `bombs' by blending, in perfect harmony, dishes and ingredients that at first sight don't go together. That in itself is a fine art. If you can do that, you're up there with the greats. Unsurprisingly, this is his motto:
`You can combine everything, you only need to find the right quantities.'
This philosophy instantly turns his cuisine into a very personal statement which makes it almost impossible for others to copy. If a dish was prepared by Pierre, you can taste it immediately. And that is why I admire him so much. It is extremely difficult to achieve the right balance in recipes such as these; you could say it is an exact science. Add one drop too many of one in-

gredient, or not enough of another one, and all of a sudden this dish, at the highest echelons of gastronomy, becomes inedible. This just shows the precision of Pierre's cooking.

When I'm out and about, I tend to take pictures of almost everything I eat. However, this is not allowed at Gagnaire's. The moment I crossed the threshold I had to surrender my camera. That did feel somewhat uncomfortable and I can't say I was happy with it. Undeterred, I decided to focus even more on the tastes and the way the various courses were structured. When we left Gaya Rive Gauche, my camera was returned to me. It contained pictures of all the dishes we had enjoyed that afternoon. That definitely makes my top-5 of the best surprises ever. This was my first, most pleasurable, encounter with this tremendous chef.

My relationship with Pierre would evolve into some sort of friendship, even though I can't say that we know each other particularly well. Pierre made a habit of sitting down with me after the meal to ask me what I thought of it. `Let's discuss the different courses, tell me what you have tasted and also tell me where I could have done better', Pierre used to ask me. In the beginning I found this a little weird and also, I wasn't quite sure how to handle it. I wanted to be politeness personified and address him with the utmost respect. And this is why I was not brave enough to cut right through to the bone. In the end, Pierre could not fail to notice and he told me: `No Bart, I really want to know what you thought of it'. We struck up many a deep conversation and Pierre even adjusted some of his recipes based on my comments. At the time this left a deep impression on me. To the extent that nowadays, I make my opinion clear from the word go. People may feel hurt, but that is never my intention. I will always give feedback on the work, not on the person responsible for it. And, if at all possible, I will give positive feedback as well so it is turned into a learning experience. Especially amongst colleagues, I am straight to the point. I won't play up to anyone just to get in their good books. That's no use to anyone.

MAURO COLAGRECO: Bart and I met for the first time at an event of a common friend. I had already heard of his fantastic cooking, but as a chef you also want to discover why it is so fantastic. Fortunately I ran into him again at a conference of Relais & Chateaux. It became a cordial and
unforgettable encounter. The kind of meeting that made me think even more about my philosophy about food.

With Pastorale he has built up a restaurant based on an incredible knowledge of the product, combined with an endless learning process. Clarabella is a good example of this. A breed of cow not exactly top of mind is transformed with so much expertise into a product to envy. That requires a lot of passion, curiosity and an indomitable drive. He is without a doubt a talented chef. Creative, entrepreneurial and with a big heart. They don't come around very often. Love it!

ANNE: When Bart came to Paris he and I had to work in close co-operation. We carried out a hotel audit as a team. Now and again we had lunch or dinner at a restaurant. This was obviously work-related as we wanted to map the local competition, but secretly I also really enjoyed our get-togethers. After Paris we carried on our email correspondence. It was always about work, but every mail had a slight undercurrent. Words that remained unsaid. In one of his emails, Bart invited me to Rumst. He wanted to show me his restaurant and share his philosophy. In brief, he wanted to explain why he did what he did and how he did it. The moment that changed everything is when Bart showed me a book about Tomorrowland. Up that point I had never heard of it. I am normally known as a big techno fan but I did not know a thing about this fantastic festival. When Bart offered me a ticket I snapped it up without a moment's hesitation.

After the festival I didn't see Bart for quite a while, but we stayed in touch through WhatsApp. One month before Tomorrowland Bart sent me a message, almost out of the blue. He was working in Lille, but the event wasn't going as well as expected. He was doing the catering in the fan zone of Lille's football team. But, with the Paris attacks a recent memory, very few people had turned up. So I sent a message back saying that Lille-Paris was only an hour by train. It wasn't long before he turned up in Paris, clutching a bottle of wine. And at that point, our friendship developed into just that little bit more.

Although we have the same star sign, we are completely different in many other ways. I tend to wait and see what happens; Bart is often full of childlike enthusiasm. If he believes in something, he really goes for it. If there are any questions or issues, he will cross that bridge when he gets to it. I may roll my eyes and look up to the heavens, but to be honest, I really like this aspect of his personality and perhaps it's what attracted me to him in the first place. That enthusiasm and that boundless energy. I sometimes wonder how you can switch him down a gear. Thinking about it, I think that's quite impossible. Also, Bart has an enormously positive approach to life. He believes in the innate goodness of people.

All told, it was a pleasure and a privilige to let him discover 'my' Paris. Or rather and in the first place, the restaurants of Paris. Having dinner with Bart does have its drawbacks. As he knows so many people and has such a large network, we were hardly ever entirely on our own. At almost every restaurant we went to, someone would come out from the kitchen to say hello. When we went for a bite to eat at Saturne I could not believe my eyes. We walk into this small, cosy restaurant. And who do we see, at one of the tables? The former sous-chef of Pastorale, his own restaurant. Paris has thousands of restaurants. What are the odds of coming across your own staff in a small restaurant in a city of millions?

All in all it took a year before I plucked up the courage to move to Rumst. I have never ever regretted it, even for a second. I just followed my heart, just like Bart has done all of his life.

Bart
POSTUUR
daily foodculture

REUBEN SANDWICH
CORNED BEEF SANDWICH
ORDER SANDWICHES HERE
MURPHY'S IRISH AMBER
KATZ'S DELICATESSEN

KATZ'S That's all!

KATZ'S
That's all!

New York 2017

BART: At first I wasn't a fan of America. I found it hard to reconcile the American way of living with my own character. I strongly associated the world across the pond with fast food and unhealthy meals.

But, as my daughter Jolien went to university in America and my wife Anne has worked there, I did end up in America at the ripe old age of 49. In New York, to be exact. The city made such an impression on me that I returned in the same year. Ask me today where I would most like to go on a city break and it's a no-brainer. The answer is the city that never sleeps.

I did not fall in love with New York straight away. The city had to put in an effort to win me over and vice versa. Lots of people, tall buildings, European designer stores... I had seen all of that in Japan and Singapore. So, I had to look beyond this. Lower East Side was the first area in New York that managed to steal my heart. I was particularly won over by the small restaurants run by creative people who managed to turn their lovely concepts into reality. So much was new to me that I embarked on my journey of discovery with great gusto.

Even the salads and healthy food went far above and beyond my expectations. Yes, fast food was in abundance, but I also came across a lot of *fast good food* that really served as an inspiration to me. And, I now want to translate this mindset and these concepts to Belgium and, who knows, spread it around Europe.

Fast good food

Healthy eating has really come under the spotlight over the past few years. I am a great supporter of this trend. In combination with our busy, day-to-day lifestyles, you just know that there is a market for *fast good food*. Food that is not only good for you, but also fits perfectly within our 'grab and go' culture. Clever, fast, efficient and sustainable are some other buzzwords used to describe Fast Good Food. Bart sees this as an interesting environment to fine-tune his culinary creations and target them at a particular audience.

Ellis Gourmet Burger

BART: When I worked for Electrolux I registered with Leaders Club Belgium. This is an association of independent business people who do more than just run a business and who get together to exchange experiences. The international character of the association had an immediate appeal for me.

At Leaders club I met Thierry Canetta of Ellis Gourmet Burger. He owns the brand and straight away, presented me with a huge challenge: make me the best burger.

Now, in my life I had made and eaten plenty of good burgers, but to produce the very best burger, that's a completely different ball game. And I am only talking about the meat that goes into it. The bun, vegetables and condiments – some of these quite literally came on top of it. Initially I thought it would be easy to give the client what he wanted. A big mistake, as it turned out. First of all it took me half a year to understand Thierry's concept of the very best burger. There's no accounting for taste, or so they say, but this hamburger had to be indisputably the best. Thierry and I travelled to Paris and London as a team to eat many, many burgers. I remember that within six hours, we popped into seven different burger joints.

If you ask me, a hamburger is a beef patty with added protein and salt. Thierry's idea of a burger was more like a steak haché, a ground steak in other words. So I focused on this and accepted the challenge to produce a machine-made steak haché. The work involved was painstaking. We turned two large machines into one bigger one with the sole purpose of making that specific hamburger for Ellis Gourmet Burger. Look, we produce over one million hamburgers for them every single year. You'd better make sure that not only the burgers, but also the machinery is of top quality.

RAW

Raw

The fourth edition of Culinaria, a 'starred' festival focusing on food and enjoyment, was held at an impressive venue: Tours and Taxis. For the first time ever, the festival had a particular theme, which on this occasion was Raw. To mark the event, Bart created a recipe with foie gras, aspic of oxtail, smoked oxtail and sour cream, finished with mustard cress, yarrow and sorrel.

The 'raw' theme was underlined by a video produced by Franky Claeys. In this short movie, a boxer is expressing his frustration about the love he lost by taking it out on a large chunk of raw meat suspended on a hook in a cold chamber. A tongue-in-cheek reference as well as a homage to Rocky, the 1980s boxing cinema icon.

TARRAGON MAYONNAISE

B-Foodie

In this modern urban jungle we are forever searching for happiness and instant gratification. This is why street food and food truck festivals are very much on the 'up' as it takes no time at all to grab a tasty bite. B-Foodie is Bart's take on fast food. He transforms it into fast good food with a green twist. Honest dishes without added nitrates or any other artificial additives. For any event. Whether you are serving burgers, hot dogs, wraps or pancakes, you always end up with a great occasion that suits your requirements perfectly. To make sure that all of these catering events would be successful, Bart more partnered up with Electrolux once more. Together they developed a panini grill that could toast a panini 75% faster, without affecting the quality. The sole purpose of this exercise was to turn fast good food into extra fast good food.

HOT DOG - MILK SANDWICH - MUSHROOMS ›

SAUERKRAUT - ONION - LARD - JUNIPER - CORIANDER SEEDS - SMOKED BACON

Tomorrowland

For Bart, Reet has been both a curse and a blessing. In the days of childhood, it was verging on Paradise. But as Bart grew up, he felt its limitations and experienced it as a source of frustration. It was time for Bart to venture out and spread his wings. Bart has always had the entrepreneurial spirit but was also gripped by the travel bug. Sometimes it takes a crisis to bring out the entrepreneur in you. 2007 saw the demise of many restaurants which prompted Bart to start thinking laterally. Bring something new to the market or go bust. It was time for Bart to spread his wings.

BART: With Pastorale we had built a great platform for ourselves. We were plating up around 10,000 dishes every year and our service was reliable like a well-oiled machine. There was one issue we were struggling with: how to apply these same quality standards to a wider audience.

And that was just the type of challenge I wanted to embrace. I was given my first opportunity by the organisers of the Tomorrowland festival. When this festival was in full swing, we used to close down the restaurant for a week. We'd take a few days off or do some maintenance. On the occasion of the festival's 10th anniversary, the organisers asked me if I would consider cooking for a select group of people in my own back yard, so to speak. They felt it wasn't right to fly in the best chefs in the world, at great expense, whereas only a few kilometres away there was another two-starred chef who might just be available. I only took a couple of seconds to consider their proposal. I declined...

... but immediately put a different proposal on the table. I wanted to cook for everyone. Not just for a select(ed) group of people, but for the entire festival. So I asked if I could bring a burger bar along. This sounds quite ordinary and down-to-earth, but nothing could be further from the truth. We unleashed a two-star philosophy on a simple hamburger. Yes, with the organisers' permission we took the humble burger to a higher plane. I knew that whatever was on offer at the festival at the time, I could do it better, faster and healthier. I set myself a goal: to bring the same Pastorale quality to the catering for a festival site, for 300,000 people, over a six-day period. I had to adopt a different way of thinking. I had to change gears very quickly. It has been a growth process for me as well. However, we used all of our accumulated knowledge, always using Pastorale as our starting point, we managed to bring this project to a great conclusion. This type of event is not for the faint-hearted. It takes humongous efforts, great organisation skills as well as a hefty dose of flexibility. 120 people worked around the clock to make this happen. The script documents every single detail, there are pictures of all the dishes. Every single detail is written down, from all the credits for everyone who helped out in any way, down to the names of those who sold the hamburgers. Nothing is left to chance. Every time, the six days of the festival leave me utterly exhausted. At the same time, my stint at Tomorrowland gives me new energy to embark on new projects and give them my all.

LIVE TODAY LOVE TOMORROW UNITE FOREVER
LAMB PLATTERS
BY BART DE POOTER
pastorale
LIVE TODAY LOVE TOMORROW UNITE FOREVER
PREMIUM BURGERS
BY BART DE POOTER
pastorale

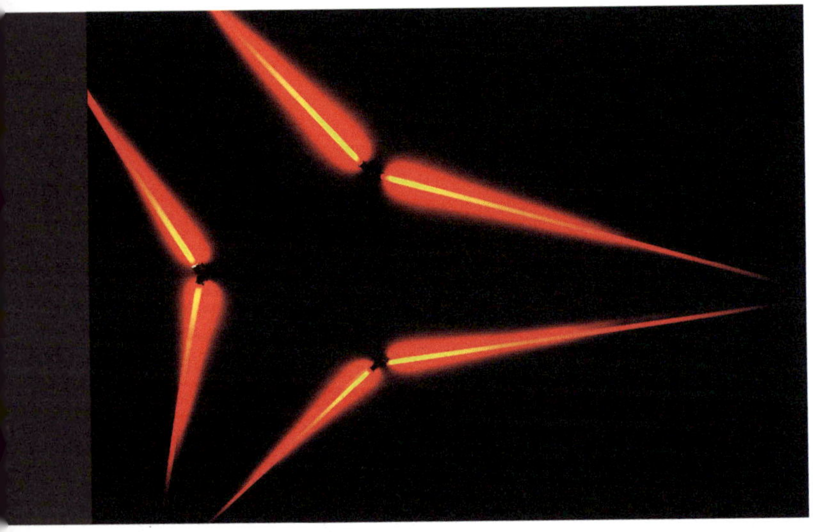

A STAR FOR A STAR

Taking Pastorale to another level **WY!** 2012

Mercedes offers Bart the opportunity to open up a restaurant at Mercedes House, located in the heart of the Sablon (Zavel) area in Brussels. Almost instantly, the concept starts to take shape in Bart's brain. It should be a type of meeting centre, but the idea of an experience centre also comes into it. There will be a restaurant, naturally, but there will also be space for exhibitions, art and culture.
The centre is given the name of WY, which first and foremost, stands for Welcome You.
The 'Y' in the name is a reference to the floor plans of The Mercedes House, based on the initial designs drawn up by architects Jo Crepain and Luc Binst. Furthermore, the 'Y' is clearly also a reference to the star in the Mercedes-Benz logo. The 'W' joined the 'Y' to represent Bart's own personal take on the project. The W stands for Why. Bart is always asking questions, of himself and others. Why is he doing this? What does he want to achieve with this new concept and where does he want to take it? The main objective is to pique the guests' curiosity and to send them home with a hefty dose of food *for the mind.*

House
BY BART DE POOTER

The kitchen, created by Electrolux to Bart's specifications, is something to behold. Not only is it completely kitted out in chrome, it comes with cameras fixed above the cooker, which instantly gives new meaning to the term 'open kitchen'. Images of every single detail of the creative process are transmitted to large LED screens fitted on the rear wall of the kitchen. We now have the ultimate form of 'show cooking', in other words, how your wider audience can quite literally see what's cooking.

When Bart took the step from the rural village of Reet to the busy city centre of Brussels, he felt it was a way to put himself, and Pastorale, on the map. To increase their presence, as it were. Pastorale came about largely by fate and co-incidence. In contrast, Bart made a deliberate choice to get involved in WY as he wanted to translate his concept of the ideal restaurant into an urban environment. He wanted to infiltrate elements of the urban character of Brussels into the Mercedes House and so he opted for graffiti, posters and neon signs for the interior design of the building. A clear plan, a clear vision and a clear execution. Throw a superior gastronomic experience into the mix and you are on to a winner. WY gained its first star only ten months after launch. An unprecedented tour de force.

POSTUUR

Bart's New York experience inspired him to set up a *fast good food* business in Belgium. ABCVegan and Chopt really fired his imagination to the extent that he felt that this particular concept would be successful in Belgium as well. Bart didn't hang about. When he had the chance to set up a genuine 'lunch room' at the Post X building in Berchem, he jumped at the opportunity. The concept was considered in depth, designs were drawn up and architects were consulted. It took many steps, some of them placed in the very concrete the building is made of, but eventually, POSTUUR saw the light.

BART: I thoroughly enjoyed the experience of translating this *healthy* mind set into a simple canteen. In theory, a canteen is just somewhere people go to eat, but at the same time, everybody is looking forward to lunch as it gives them a break from their day. I looked into the typical issues of your standard canteen: uncomfortable seating, long queues, poor quality food most of the time... I felt that I could approach it in quite a different way. Fresh from my experience at Tomorrowland I started to work with Paul Gelders to cobble together Canteen version 2.0. Where, just like at Tomorrowland, you could sit down at a particular kiosk, with many to choose from. One kiosk for rolls and sandwiches, one for flat breads, one for pasta... It would be a place where you would find all sorts of *niet cursief* preparations, from simple sandwiches to stews, but you would also be able to buy healthy salads or meat from the grill. All of this made with selected, high quality products. Furthermore, we will only use products with a 100% guaranteed provenance. The wheat, the meat, the vegetables, and what have you. Yes, for every single item we know where it comes from and how it is produced. It is a warm, welcoming and convivial environment that is more than just fit for purpose. The overall experience was just as important. POSTUUR aims to be a welcoming environment that puts the client's experience at the centre. I am fortunate in that I have a great team, made up of 20 people, under the capable management of my daughter and Anne. They make sure that everything is as it should be and allow me to keep my finger on the pulse of POSTUUR.

PAUL GELDERS: Bart is a top chef who, at Tomorrowland, gained much experience with catering for the masses. What's more, he achieved this with fast good food. He is one of very few chefs in Belgium who managed to do this. Not only at Tomorrowland, but also at other major events. We will work with Bart to build and expand POSTUUR to make it into a canteen fit for the 22nd century. Our story will be healthy and sustainable. From clothing to packaging and anything in between. And to make all of this happen, the best partner to have is one who shares your mindset.

PASCAL VINDEVOGEL, B2B-ADVISOR BELFIUS:

I met Bart through his accountant, whom I have known professionally for a long time. She introduced me to Bart and before long, we struck up a great business relationship. What I really like about Bart is that he has a clear vision and philosophy for every single project he takes on: to deliver a product of the highest quality that adds value to and enhances his clients' business. Also, Bart is driven to such an extent that he will do everything in his power to make this happen.

Almost all of Bart's projects flow into one another in a natural, you could almost say organic, way. Cross-fertilisation is the term that springs to mind. From Pastorale, where Bart serves meals of the highest quality, via his beef import business down to his work as a consultant to fellow entrepreneurs active in different sectors of the food business. His talents extend to Tomorrowland, where he has found a very quick way to fill many empty stomachs with his hamburgers à la Bart and other good fast food. Above all I would like to say that Bart is always aiming for the highest quality. That could be with the works of art at Pastorale of in a field 200 metres away from his business.

His most recent project is Postuur, at the Post X Business Park in Antwerp. This is the perfect symbiosis of Bart's entrepreneurial spirit, his passion to offer added value to his meals, his drive and his experience at Pastorale (slow enjoyment) and Tomorrowland (very fast enjoyment). Providing a 'company canteen' at the Post X Business Park, really the size of a small village, with high quality food that exceeds the usual standards, is another string to Bart's bow. An achievement that clients will appreciate for the value it adds to their business.

We at Belfius feel it is of great importance to support businessmen like Bart in turning his plans into reality. Our bank is 100% Belgian and we are keen on providing guidance to entrepreneurs in all matters related to finance and insurance, both on a personal and a professional basis. Just like Bart, we have a clear vision on where we want to go and have the same drive and passion to add value to the client's business. But we also have to be a good match, which we had with Bart straight away.

Bart is a perfectionist in everything, and puts high demands on his bankers, but he is never unrealistic in his expectations. That stands to reason, otherwise you never reach the high level where he is now, with all of his different projects.

His perfectionism extends to his relationships with people: his word is his word.

Also, as a person, he has a lot of empathy. He is someone who notices the human being behind the banker. Bart shows this in every contact he has, whether with his staff, suppliers or customers. As far as I am concerned, that human touch, in pairing with his drive and focus, makes Bart the equivalent of an extremely pleasant collaboration with a top businessman.

One happy team

"A kitchen is not created by a recipe. A kitchen is created by a team, a constant factor, a philosophy and a personality."

Sharing is caring

I don't mind being copied. There's absolutely nothing wrong with it. I view it as a sign of respect, to show me that I am doing well and that other people are interested in what I am up to. Also, I like to spread my knowledge around. I am very happy to share my techniques and experiences for others to use. For me, to cook is to share with colleagues.

As to me, I try to take advantage of my strong points: I will never cease to be inquisitive or to develop things; I will continue to play around with the seasons which are different every year. This combination keeps me on my toes and leads to further discoveries.

Pastorale
By Bart De Poot

AM ONE PHIL
One Team
1

One Team

The future

BART: I worked my socks off to reach the top of the world of gastronomy. If I carry on as I am, cooking the very best food, served with top-quality beverages in a superb ambience, perhaps one day I will get there. That would be my ultimate ambition, and who knows, one day my dream will come true.
Pastorale is only a small part of my business. These days I work from quite a broad platform. It has been my great good fortune to be able to sample so many things, literally as well as figuratively. And now I have my children, who support me in the business. If I needed any more motivation, they are it.

Bart has two daughters. Jolien, his elder daughter, was born in 1993 and trained as a chef at Hotelschool Ter Duinen. Further educational stints included the Hotel Management School at Maastricht followed by the Ecole Hôtelière at Lausanne where she gained her Master's Degree of Global Hospitality. Jolien spent a year working at the Crowne Plaza Brussels Airport before she joined her father's business, Post X: POSTUUR, as a floor manager.
Karen is Bart's younger daughter, born in 1995. Karen attended Sint-Lukas College in Antwerp before swopping this city for Hasselt University where she read architecture. After one year she flocked back to the nest in Antwerp where she continued her architectural studies. She is now welcoming the guests at Pastorale.

JOLIEN: My Dad has always been quite strict on me and my sister. Yes, rules were rules, but he was also honest and fair. He always tried to encourage us to be the best we could be. Not unlike Dad himself, I think. But, above all, he was and still is a very loving and caring father.
Life hasn't always been easy, but when you take a look at what I have already achieved in my short life and where I am today, most of this I owe to Bart, my Dad. He has always helped me to pick the very best schools and places to work so, throughout my life, I had the very best education. At home we were also spoilt when it came to food. Or, you could say we were educated. I remember that at a young age, we went to the farm on a school visit and we were served mashed potato. After one mouthful I exclaimed to my friends 'Yuk, it doesn't have any nutmeg in it.' No-one else felt that was a problem. This led me to feel that I was a picky eater. Nothing could be further from the truth. I simply love good food. I learned that at my father's knee.
From when we were little, whenever we were eating out at a restaurant, we always had to wait for a particular course to finish before we were allowed to take out our games or colouring books. We had to wait till after the first course and this gradually became longer. Once we had passed the 'play' stage, we used to help Papa with taking pictures and making notes. We were always seen as lovely, very obedient children.
Also in Quiberon, where I did my traineeship, taste beat logic hand over fist. On my very last day my parents came to help me pack and tidy up. Early in the morning I popped to the baker's with Papa. The idea was that we would get a quick breakfast together so we could get back to work. Easier said than done. We were walking past a market with fresh produce and each and every stall had to be inspected. To make a long story short: we returned a few hours' later, bearing four kilograms of seafood. Yes, that was our breakfast, but it would also turn into our lunch and evening meal.
Before my traineeship at Quiberon and also when I was studying for my Master's, I did various stints at my Dad's businesses. When I was only about fifteen I helped out at Pastorale on the customer side of things. And how did this come about? At a particular point in time I told my Dad that I wanted to be a sommelier. I was really bad at geography but I was determined that this was the career I was going for. True to his word, Dad let me work at Pastorale during my time off from school. He gave me the job so I could learn the tricks of the trade, but he also wanted me to find out for myself if the world of wining and dining would suit me.

When Papa took me with him to Hong Kong, one evening we had dinner in a small restaurant just above the fish market. Papa, who was already reasonably familiar with Asian culture, ordered the most 'unusual' food, definitely not what you would expect from a European: fish heads, chicken claws, and so on. The owner of the business, who spoke some English, asked Daddy if he knew what he had ordered. They had never come across this situation before. Well, we ordered a huge amount so we could taste as many different dishes as we possibly could.
When we are on holiday, it's a given that we will make an effort to sample the flavours of the traditional cuisine. We avoid touristy restaurants so we can have a sniff at the authentic local cuisine and culture.
Taste life... yes, it sounds like the biggest cliché around. But with a two-star chef for a Dad, it is also the biggest truth there is.
We don't always have to talk about food so I would like to add one last comment: Papa never ever lets anyone beat him when we play a game. No way. Apart from that, he is just a great human being.

KAREN: Papa is a stickler for the rules. Some people may call him strict, severe even, but I don't usually get that impression. He will only ever make a comment when one is needed. And also in such a way that you understand it and learn from it. But apart from that, he is very loving, caring as well as spontaneous.

What I will never forget as long as I live, is that on his day off he came into my school, Eikenlaar in Reet, to cook lunch. What he did for that school, completely voluntarily, is something you cannot take for granted. He installed an almost professional kitchen, planted a vegetable garden and made sure that many children could enjoy tasty and healthy meals. He worked with the school to introduce a vegetable day, a frites day, an 'eat-healthy-at-school' day. I really enjoyed those days.

Dad was always busy at Pastorale, but if he had any time to spare, he always made a special effort to be there for his family.

Let's be honest: if there was food around, it could get boring for us. For example, Papa often dined out at top-of-the-range, posh restaurants and invited (read: wanted) us to come along. They had a little trick to keep us quiet: colouring books. We used to love colouring in. But we were not given those colouring books without doing something in return. When we very little, we got the books after our starter. When we were a bit older we were only given them after the main course and when we had grown up even more, the books came out after dessert. This training carried on over many years. But, it did have results. Everybody said how lovely and well-behaved we were. However, it's not always fun to take your kids to a restaurant. We once took the Eurostar to London. Papa had spent a lot of time and effort to book a table at a two-star restaurant. But as soon as we were seated and ready to eat, tiredness got the better of us. The two-star chef had made eggs and spinach especially for my sister and me. But even before the food was served, both of us were in the land of Nod.

Even though food sometimes created a distance between us, a meal is also a great way to bring the family together. Every Sunday we all do our very best to join the family at the table. It's usually Mama who does the cooking, or Papa on special occasions. We always look forward to this family time. When he was working during the week he always made sure that he had his dinner at home. We thought that was great and I guess that it gave him a break from his busy day. Yes, our childhood was far from average, but if you look at us now and see how well things have worked for us and that we have such a great relationship with Papa, you can only be very grateful and treasure the memories.

Acknowledgement

An acknowledgement often goes unacknowledged as there are always people you forget to acknowledge. Let's get back to basics and honour the person for whom this book was written: my mother. Apart from giving me life, she has helped to shape my life and has brought me to where I am now. She has always been by my side and has given me the space to create my own biotope. Often as a driving force, but even more often as my rock in a tempestuous sea. I owe her a great deal. Without her, I would not be where I am now.

I would also like to thank Anne and my daughters Jolien and Karen from the bottom of my heart. They inspire me every day and remind me why I am doing what I am doing. Thanks to them I am eager for what is yet to come. I often see myself in them.

I have also had the great good fortune to enjoy the company and support of the many lovely people I have come across in my first five decades on this planet. Those who helped me at Pastorale and supported my other business ventures but first and foremost, the people who were my rock and kept me on an even keel in my private life. You gave me that little push just when I needed it but, when I was going too fast, you told me to take it down a gear or two. You shared my enthusiasm, when I was in high spirits and confident I could re-invent the world of cooking, but you also kept an eye on me to make sure my youthful spirits did not run away with me. You know who you are. I am grateful to all of you.

Finally, a word to all the young chefs, amateur cooks and those who just enjoy good food. Above all, use this book as a source of inspiration. Try your hand at the recipes, use them in your own way and create your own biotope. That would be my greatest pleasure. A biotope, by virtue of the word, is a unique environment. You are the only one that can decide how to create your own biotope and how, as a person or individual, you can achieve inner growth. Take my advice. Surround yourself with the right people, just like I did, and you will find that you develop a taste for life.

Thank you so much.

Register

The register includes a wide range of recipes, mainly for sides and complementary dishes.
They are categorised based on their structure.
Please use these recipes as a source of inspiration, incorporate them into a new recipe and let your own creativity shine through.

Croquants, caramels and similar

DESCRIPTION	AMOUNT	INGREDIENTS	HOW TO PREPARE	PG
Croquant of beef	500 g	beef brisket	Cut the brisket of beef into cubes measuring 8 x 8 centimetres.	117
	125 g	soy sauce	Vacuum with the soy sauce, fish sauce, sugar and salt.	
	85 g	fish sauce	Chill and marinate for 48 hours.	
	14 g	sugar	Remove the meat from the bag and pat dry.	
	6 g	salt	Cook in the microwave until completely dry and ready for use.	
			Pull apart until you are left with only very thin fibres and deep-fry them at a temperature of 180 °C.	
			Add salt to taste.	
HIT ME **Croquant of Isomalt**	600 g	fondant (mix of sugar, glucose syrup and water)	Boil the first three ingredients up to 165 °C.	63
	300 g	glucose syrup	Pour into a silicone baking tray and allow to set.	
	300 g	Isomalt	Chop roughly, then pour into the Thermomix to produce a fine powder.	
	20 g	dried blackcurrant, ground	Add the ground blackcurrant.	
			With the use of a sieve, spread a layer of this powder onto a silicon baking tray and return to the oven, at 200 °C, until the sugar melts again.	
			Once firm, store in a dry and tightly sealed container.	
Truffle meringue	150 g	egg white	Pre-heat the oven to 75 °C.	
	30 g	sugar	Whisk the egg whites with the sugar to form peaks.	
	50 g	winter truffle, finely chopped	Fold the truffle pieces into the mixture and spread out thinly onto a silicone baking sheet.	
			Dry the meringue in the pre-heated oven for approx. 5 hours, or until dry.	

Jus, infusions, bouillons, fonds, sauces

DESCRIPTION	AMOUNT	INGREDIENTS	HOW TO PREPARE	PG
Mole with dark chocolate This sauce is based on plain chocolate which accounts for its deep and dark character.	2 g	mace	Place the mace, cinnamon and cloves in a cheese cloth and tie with string so the spices can easily be removed from the casserole after cooking.	141
	9	sticks of cinnamon	Place the bag, together with the other ingredients, in a large casserole on the hob and bring to the boil. Thicken for 4 to 5 hours on low heat.	
	0,5 g	cloves	Remove the bag with the spices from the casserole. Finely blend into a sauce and sieve before use. Perfect in combination with lamb.	
	2 liter	water		
	400 g	butter		
	200 g	onion		
	75 g	pecan nut		
	200 g	plain chocolate		
	20 g	pumpkin seeds		
	20 g	garlic		
	42 g	salt		
	3 g	dried chili peppers, de-seeded		
	10 g	sesame seed		
	5 g	cumin		
	5 g	coriander		
	5 g	savory (herb)		
	5 g	thyme		
	50 g	tomato paste		
	500 g	potatoes, peeled		
	50 g	cornflour		
	15 g	black garlic		

DESCRIPTION	AMOUNT	INGREDIENTS	HOW TO PREPARE	PG
Tarragon mayonnaise	350 g	mayonnaise	Mix in the Thermomix until a smooth blend is achieved.	202
	80 g	green mustard with tarragon		
	10 g	green Tabasco		
	30 g	tarragon, chopped finely		
	15 g	sushi vinegar		
Amanatsu vinaigrette	3 litres	water	First prepare a stock with crab shells. Add all the ingredients for the stock to a large pot and simmer for 3 hours. Pass through a sieve. Prepare the vinaigrette. Using a measuring jug, mix all the ingredients apart from the xanthan gum. At this point, add the xanthan gum. Emulsify the vinaigrette with a hand blander and sieve before use.	120
For the crab stock	5	crab shells		
	1	red pepper		
	1	bulb of fennel		
	1	onion		
	¼	celeriac		
	1 g	black peppercorns		
	1 g	coriander seed		
	200 ml	Noilly Prat		
	3	cloves of garlic		
	20 g	tarragon		
	20 g	thyme		
For the vinaigrette	500 ml	crab stock		
	50 ml	sushi vinegar		
	50 ml	sake		
	20 ml	amanatsu juice		
	20 ml	rice vinegar		
	20 ml	lime juice		
	20 ml	dashi vinegar		
	10 ml	saltwater		
	1,5 g	xanthan gum		
Jus of plankton	750 ml	clear apple juice from Granny Smiths	Stir well and sieve the mixture.	135
	2,5 g	ascorbic acid		
	125 ml	juice of white cabbage		
	125 ml	juice of savoy cabbage		
	3 g	plankton powder		
Bouillon with infusion of cedar	5 kg	chicken bones	By first making a stock (bouillon) before infusing it, you can easily bring a particular ingredient to the fore within a dish. As an example, here is a bouillon with cedar wood. Bring all of the ingredients to the boil, apart from the cedar wood shavings and simmer on low heat for two hours. Sieve the stock. Season with salt.	72-3
For the chicken stock	8 litres	of water		
	600 g	celery		
	3	carrots		
	2	large onions		
	2,5 g	juniper berries		
	15 g	salt		
	7 g	cedar wood, shaved		

Fermentation

DESCRIPTION	AMOUNT	INGREDIENTS	HOW TO PREPARE	PG
Pickled guava	4 25 g 40 g 2 g	guava fruits, seeds removed, the pink flesh cut into 0.5 mm slices sushi vinegar elderflower vinegar salt	Bring the ingredients to the boil and cool down. Vacuum the guava slices with the liquid and pickle for one week at least.	176
Fermented asparagus	2 litres 1 kg 40 g	water white asparagus salt	Put everything in a jar and seal airtight. Allow to ferment for at least 2 weeks. Use the liquid to make a sauce. Add a dash of chicken broth and mount with butter. Serve, for example, with a vegetarian dish with different sorts of carrots, tubers and turnips, in combination with wild herbs. Cut the asparagus into small pieces and mix into a salad to add an extra dimension to the taste.	
Fermented kiwi	1 kg 2 litres 40 g	peeled kiwis water salt	Put everything in a jar and seal airtight. Leave to rest and ferment for at least 1 month. Use the liquid for sauces or dressings, for example in a fennel salad. Use the kiwis to make a cream or dipping sauce, or add a little of the cream to paste and serve it with different shellfish (razor, cockle, vongole). Also delicious in combination with dill, horseradish or lardo.	
Fermented tomatillo	1 kg 2 litres 50 g	tomatillos water salt 20 basil leaves	Put everything in a jar and seal airtight. Leave to rest and ferment for at least 3 weeks. Both the tomatillos and the liquid can be used perfectly for various preparations. For example, chop the tomatillos into pieces and cook to a compote with sugar and basil. Great with cheese or as a dip. Turn the liquid into a vinaigrette with lime and basil oil. Serve over a tomato salad.	
Fermented green strawberries	1 kg 1 litre 20 g	green strawberries water salt	Put everything in a jar and seal airtight. Leave to rest and ferment for at least 4 weeks. After fermenting, the strawberries are very soft and ideal for mixing into a puree. In this way you actually create a kind of strawberry boshi, similar to the Japanese ume-boshi or sour plum paste. Stew thinly sliced cabbage with butter and a shredded shallot, and add pasta. Let it cook slowly and add some cooked pearl barley. Combine with the cabbage. Add to taste: freshly grated ginger, mirin, salt and pepper.	157
Kimchi	6 1 litre 100 g 30 g 2 g 4 g	Chinese cabbage water rice flour zout chili powder ginger powder	Cut the bottom of the cabbage and divide into leaves, or cut a cabbage into 4 parts. Mix all other ingredients together and pour over the cabbage. Rub in the mixture and between the leaves of the cabbage so that everything is well covered. Put everything in a large pot and let ferment; it is at its best in 4 weeks. Cut the cabbage into pieces and serve, for example, with a salad with radishes and lemon, or with carrot and shiso leaves, also delicious with ramen noodles.	155

Ice cream, granités, sorbets, ice cream powders and other side dishes

DESCRIPTION	AMOUNT	INGREDIENTS	HOW TO PREPARE	PG
Shiso ice cream	350 g	water	Boil the ingredients listed under A and place in the fridge to set for 12 hours.	102
A:	300 g	coconut milk	Mix in the Thermomix and add the ingredients under B.	
	180 g	sugar	Freeze in Pacojet containers.	
	80	saké		
	4 g	gellan		
B:	45 g	yuzu juice		
	30 g	green shiso leaves		
Topinambur ice cream	200 g	milk	Vacuum the milk, cream, topinambur and sugar and heat sous-vide at 95 °C for 40 minutes.	100
	300 g	cream	Then blend into a puree with the Xanthan gum, gelatine and ice cream emulsifier. Push through a fine sieve and freeze in Pacojet containers.	
	400 g	topinambur, peeled		
	80 g	sugar		
	2 g	Xanthan gum		
	2 leaves	gelatine		
	50 g	ice cream emulsifier		
Granité of truffles	3 leaves	gelatine	Steep the gelatine leaves in cold water.	
	35 g	sugar	Add the other ingredients to the Thermomix to produce a smooth blend.	
	385 g	mineral water	Melt the gelatine in a small quantity of the mixture.	
	7 g	glucose	Add to the remaining mixture and whizz in the Thermomix for a short while.	
	70 g	winter truffle	Pour into a large container and place in the freezer.	
	2 g	truffle oil	Stir the mixture with a fork every 30 minutes to make the shavings.	
	4 g	lemon juice		
	4 g	squid ink		
Vanilla ice cream with ginger cake	120 g	egg yolk	Make the vanilla ice cream. Loosely whisk the egg yolk with the sugar.	107
For the vanilla ice cream:	140 g	sugar	Bring the other ingredients to the boil and blend.	
	2 litres	of milk	Simmer briefly to cook through.	
	250 ml	cream	Transfer to Pacojet containers and freeze.	
	3	vanilla pods	Prepare the ginger cake. Blend all of the ingredients into a smooth dough, bake in a shallow tin at	
	15 g	gellan gum	160 °C for around 60 minutes or until done.	
For the ginger cake:	250 g	butter, creamed	Check by inserting a wooden skewer until it comes out clean.	
	900 g	honey	Turn the cake into crumbs and dry for about 4 hours at 80 °C. Turn regularly.	
	6	eggs	Use the Thermomix to prepare a fine crumble.	
	500 g	flour	Express the frozen ice cream from the Pacojet to make small dumplings, also known as quenelles. Roll the quenelles through the ginger cake crumble.	
	12 g	bicarbonate of soda	Put back in the freezer and cut in half just before serving.	
	10 g	powdered cinnamon		
	10 g	powdered ginger		
	10 g	powdered aniseed		

Side dishes with chocolate

DESCRIPTION	AMOUNT	INGREDIENTS	HOW TO PREPARE	PG
Golden truffle	1 litre	calamansi juice	For the ganache.	232-3
For the ganache:	1 litre	orange juice	Reduce the juices until you are left with 750 grams.	
	15 g	spice mix for 'speculaas'	Add the speculaas spice mix.	
	1,5 kg	milk chocolate	Melt the chocolate.	
To finish off:	800 g	milk chocolate	Emulsify the ganache into a smooth mixture by adding small quantities of liquid to the chocolate, stirring all the time with a spatula. Careful!	
	80 g	cocoa butter 'callets', or drops	Stir gently so you don't introduce air into the ganache.	
	100 g	cocoa powder	If any air does creep into the ganache, remove it by blending with a hand-held blender at the bottom of the saucepan.	
	10 g	powdered gold	When you can barely hear the mixer, the ganache is air-free. Pipe the ganache into silicon cake pop moulds and freeze at -30 °C. To finish off, melt the milk chocolate with 10 percent cocoa butter and, using a fork, dip the balls into the mixture. Immediately coat in cocoa powder with a little powdered gold mixed in.	

Fish, meat and shellfish

DESCRIPTION	AMOUNT	INGREDIENTS	HOW TO PREPARE	PG
Terrine of foie gras	50 g	whisky	Flambé the whisky, the white port and the Madeira in a casserole to make the alcohol evaporate.	68-9
	25 g	white port	Blend the foie gras with the sel rouge, pepper, cinnamon and the cassonade in a mixing bowl and smoke twice over, using cedar wood.	
	25 g	Madeira	Heat a spoon until red-hot. Place in a deep tray next to the foie gras and sprinkle on the cedar powder. Quickly cover the tray with aluminium foil so no smoke is lost.	
	400 g	foie gras, pan-fried	Wait until all of the smoke has disappeared. Then, push the foie into a terrine mould and steam at 65 °C for 40 minutes.	
	6 g	sel rouge	Cool down completely and allow to firm up before turning upside down.	
	1 g	black pepper, ground	Cut into beautiful slices and add salt if desired.	
	0,2 g	cinnamon powder		
	10 g	dark cassonade sugar		
	0,2 g	cedar powder		
Soft shell crab tempura		oil for frying	Heat the oil up to 180 °C.	
	300 ml	vodka	Mix the vodka, rice flour, flour and sparkling water using a whisk and a sieve.	
	300 g	rice flour	Pour the batter into a syphon and aerate with two cartridges.	
	300 g	flour	Rest for 15 minutes.	
	500 ml	sparkling water	Spray into a mixing bowl and pass the crab through the batter. Gently lower the crab into the oil and deep-fry until the batter takes on a lovely hue of golden-brown. Add salt to taste	
	1	softshell crab, cleaned		

Fish matured in kombu — 175

To serve on the side: butterhead lettuce/mimolette cheese/buckwheat
This is where salt is added to the hiramasa immediately after filleting. Instead of letting the salt permeate the fish, we cover one side of the fillet with kombu/vinegar leaves.
We allow two days before enjoying our fish. Carve diagonally into thin slices, making sure the kombu layer remains intact.

DESCRIPTION	AMOUNT	INGREDIENTS	HOW TO PREPARE	PG
Skrei matured in miso	150 g 50 g 100 g 800 g	shiro miso ginger syrup saké fillet of skrei, skin removed	Whisk up the shiro miso, the ginger syrup and the saké. Pour the mixture into a tray and place the fillet of skrei on top. Go easy on the salt, in fact, you don't need it. The shiro miso concoction does much the same thing. Mature for at least 1 week.	156
Barbecued Mackerel	150 g 150 g 150 g 10 g 150 g	sushi vinegar ginger syrup dark soy sauce dried bonito flakes mackerel for each diner	To make the glaze, bring the sushi vinegar to the boil together with the ginger syrup, the dark soy sauce and the bonito flakes and reduce (by half, approximately), to achieve a consistency that you like. Cool down. Fillet the mackerel and remove the skin. Add salt as above, 8 grams of salt per 1 kg of fish. Cut the fish into portions as desired and insert heat-proof skewers. Place directly on the hot coals - do not use a grill. Baste with the glaze every 60 seconds. Depending on the temperature and how well cooked you like your mackerel, the fish will be ready anytime between 2 to 4 minutes.	128-9
Glazed sardine	150 g 150 g 150 g 10 g 40 g	sushi vinegar ginger syrup dark soy sauce dried bonito flakes sardines per person	To prepare the glaze, bring the sushi vinegar to the boil together with the ginger syrup, the dark soy sauce and the bonito flakes. Reduce to a lovely thick consistency (by about half). Cool down. Remove the bones and scales from the sardines. Add salt as before, 8 gr salt per 1 kilogram of fish. Baste the fish using the glaze and place under the grill for a short time. Baste once more before serving. Please note, do not add any more salt! The glaze lends a perfect flavour to the fish.	137
Barbecued oysters	75 g 25 g 50 g 50 g 5 g 1 g 25 g 12	fresh lime juice sushi vinegar celery seed oil charcoal oil sugar salt finely diced brunoise of granny smith apples oysters celery leaves to garnish	To make the vinaigrette, blend the lime juice, the sushi vinegar, the celery oil, the charcoal oil, the sugar and the salt. Add the apple brunoise. Shuck the oysters, detach them from their shells. Retain the juices contained within the shells. Go for the very best quality of oyster and also, buy the biggest you can get as oysters do tend to shrink when they are cooked. Place your particular 'flat' oysters on the grill, just above the hot coal fire. Grill for about 2 minutes. Make sure they don't spend too much time on the grill. Your oysters will be overcooked and tough. Remove from the grill and add a spoonful of vinaigrette to the shell. Serve warm and garnish with celery leaves.	130-1
How to cook a lobster	1 20 g	raw lobster tail, freshly shelled lemon oil	Vacuum the tail with the oil. Cook sous-vide until done; Almost cooked: 46 °C Easy to eat: 54 °C Firm: 59 °C The lobster tail is ready when its core had reached the desired temperature. Use a thermometer to check.	121

DESCRIPTION	AMOUNT	INGREDIENTS	HOW TO PREPARE	PG

Dim sum

DESCRIPTION	AMOUNT	INGREDIENTS	HOW TO PREPARE	PG
Dim sum duck For the stuffing:	80 g 50 g 5 g 25 g 0,3 g 0,7 g 40 g 1,5 g 20 g 3 g 0,5 g 0,5 g	duck confit (to make duck confit, sous-vide for 4 hours at 85 °C), diced finely artichoke, cut into a small brunoise black bean sauce plum sauce five spice Xanthan gum chicken stock salt celery, cut into a small brunoise lime juice chilli powder lime zest Dim sum sheets	Mix all of the ingredients until they form a coherent mass. Spoon the mixture onto dim sum sheets, moisten the edges and fold into the desired shape. Heat a little oil in a frying pan. Bake the bottom of the dim sum until crispy. Add a little water to the frying pan – you don't need much – then cover with a lid and steam the dim sum until ready. Remove the lid and let the remaining water evaporate so the dim sum turns crispy again.	

Bread, cake and so on

DESCRIPTION	AMOUNT	INGREDIENTS	HOW TO PREPARE	PG
Fennel bread	10 g 7 g 7 g 2 kg 50 g 100 g 50 g 75 g 1,65 kg	fennel seed aniseed mustard seed flour salt butter fresh yeast bread improving agent fresh fennel juice	Heat the oven to a temperature of 190 °C. Grind all the spices into a fine powder. Using a kneading machine, blend all of the ingredients into a finely composed dough (4 minutes on slow, 6 minutes on a fast setting). Throw around the dough ball to add elasticity and rest for 30 minutes. Divide the dough into 450 g segments and flip over to allow air to enter. Use to fill a greased baking tin, allow to rise for 50 minutes at a very low temperature of 32 °C and add liquid as required. Place the bread into the pre-heated oven. After 10 minutes, lower the temperature to 180 °C and bake for another 25 to 30 minutes.	114
Marzipan waffles For the waffles (galettes):	500 g 25 g 1 250 ml 25 ml 40 g 8 g 75 g	flour fresh yeast egg milk milk sugar salt glucose	Make a smooth batter with the flour, the fresh yeast, the egg and 225ml of milk. Rest for half an hour. Melt the other 25ml of milk with the sugar, the salt and the glucose and mix in with the batter. Finally, add the butter and process into a soft, smooth dough. Prove for a further 30 minutes. Roll into balls of 180 gram each, which will make 15 galettes. Bake the galettes in a waffle iron at 200 °C.	159
For the chocolate filling:	200 g 100 g 35 g	butter, creamed marzipan egg white	Using a cutter to make sure that all of the waffles have a uniform shape. Blend the marzipan with the egg white.	
For the pistachio:	50 g 100 g 20 g	plain chocolate marzipan egg white	Melt the chocolate. Add the chocolate and mix in well with the marzipan.	
For the kirsch:	50 g 150 g 15 g 15 g	pistachio paste marzipan egg white kirsch	Blend the marzipan with the egg white. Add the pistachio paste and mix in well. Blend the marzipan with the egg white. Add the liqueur and mix in well with the marzipan.	

DESCRIPTION	AMOUNT	INGREDIENTS	HOW TO PREPARE	PG
Carrot cake	2 125 g 15 g 10 g 170 g 25 g 10 g 5 g 4 g 270 g	eggs sugar grapeseed oil hazelnut oil ground almonds flour baking powder powdered ginger ground cardamom grated carrots	Beat the eggs, the sugar, the grapeseed oil and the hazelnut oil until the mixture turns frothy. Fold in the almond powder, the flour, the baking powder, the powdered ginger and the ground cardamom. Finally, using a spatula, fold the grated carrots into the dough. Pour into a shallow baking tray covered with baking powder. Bake for 25 minutes at 160 °C.	102
Veggie burger	1100 g 20 g 50 g 75 g 100 g 100 g 100 g 20 g 580 g	flour salt yeast lard celeriac, brunoise carrot, brunoise spinach dill water	Mix everything in a blender. Then turn into a fine dough (4 minutes slowly, 6 minutes fast). Spread the ball of dough and let it rest for 30 minutes. Divide the dough into pieces of 90 gram. Form balls and place on greased baking trays. Let rise for 50 minutes at a steady 32 ° C with sufficient moisture. Place the loaves in the oven at 180 °C. Bake in 14 minutes to a golden crust.	
Verbena chocolate cake For the cake mixture:	375 g 330 g 375 g 300 g 115 g 250 g 500 g 250 g	butter sugar plain chocolate, melted eggs flour baking-resistant chocolate drops plain chocolate cocoa butter a sprinkling of dried verbena powder	Pre-heat the oven to 170 °C. Process the butter, sugar, melted chocolate, eggs and flour into a smooth mixture and add the baking-resistant chocolate drops. Cover a baking tray with baking paper and pour the mixture into it. Smooth out and bake for 22 minutes in the pre-heated oven. Turn out onto a flat sheet and freeze. Cut into cubes the size of dice. Store in the freezer. Melt the 500 grams of plain chocolate with the cocoa butter. Coat the dice with the chocolate and cocoa butter, and add a sprinkling of dried verbena powder to finish off.	104-5
Truffle cake	10 g 3 220 g 100 g 7 g 50 g 140 g 10 g 10 g	truffle shavings eggs beurre noisette trisol salt dried fungi, ground into a powder flour baking powder dark malt	Pre-heat the oven to 180 °C. Finely chop the truffle shavings. Blend the remaining ingredients until smooth and add the bits of truffle. Pipe onto silicon mats in the size of your choice, preferably a round with a diameter of 5 centimetres at the most. Bake in the pre-heated oven for approx. 6 minutes or until done.	78

Friand with pine nuts

AMOUNT	INGREDIENTS
225 g	sugar
225 g	powdered almond
100 g	caster sugar
75 g	flour
200 g	butter, melted
275 g	egg white

Pre-heat the oven to 180 °C.
Blend all the ingredients until smooth.
Pour into a piping bag and use it to fill small oval silicon moulds, with a thickness of approx. 1 centimetre.
Place 5 or 6 pine nuts on each friand.
Bake for 7 minutes in the pre-heated oven.

Chickpea taco

AMOUNT	INGREDIENTS
100 g	chickpea flour
20 g	egg yolk
10 g	cornflour
20 g	flour
220 g	water
2 g	salt
1 g	Oaxaca

Mix into a smooth dough using a hand blender.
Pass through a sieve to remove any remaining lumps.
Heat a frying pan with a solid base and grease with a little oil or cooking spray.
Fry the tacos as you would do a pancake: on either side and until done.

PG 92

Confits

Candied fruits

AMOUNT	INGREDIENTS
6	pears
6	apples
2 litres	water
40 g	Calx
2 litres	water
660 g	sugar
2 star	anise
2	cloves
2 litres	water
660 g	sugar
10	green cardamom, crushed
1	stem of lemon grass

Peal the pears and apples. Add the Calx to the 2 litres of water. Pour over the pears and apples and steep for 3 hours, stirring continuously.
Thoroughly wash the pears and apples.
Make the syrup for the pears with 2 litres of water, 660 grams of sugar, the star anise and the cloves.
Make the syrup for the apples with 2 litres of water, 660 grams of sugar, the cardamom and the lemon grass. Simmer the pears and apples in their own syrup for 3 hours, with a sheet of baking paper on top of the casserole.
Remove the fruit from the liquid and dry for 24 hours at 60 °C.

PG 142

Poached entire tangerine

AMOUNT	INGREDIENTS
1 litre	tangerine juice
500 g	water
100 g	lemon juice
250 g	honey
150 g	sugar
	zest of 3 oranges
	zest of 1 lemon
20 g	powdered liquorice
6	tangerines

Boil all of the ingredients with the exception of the tangerines and infuse for 30 minutes.
Peel the tangerines. Vacuum the tangerines with plenty of juice and infuse for 30 minutes at 60 °C.

PG 106

Caramel milk

Boil a tin of condensed milk for three hours at 100 °C. Cool down and open the tin.
Use a piping bag to make it easier to use the caramel.

Small cakes

DESCRIPTION	AMOUNT	INGREDIENTS	HOW TO PREPARE	PG
Macarons with star anise	5 400 g 400 g 20 g	eggs caster sugar flour star anise, ground sugar	Pre-heat the oven to 155 °C. Whisk the eggs and caster sugar into a froth. Sieve the flour and star anise powder and fold into the frothy eggs. Pipe small dollops onto a silicon baking mat and sprinkle with sugar. Allow to dry for 2 hours. Then, bake for 10 minutes in the pre-heated oven. Remove from the oven and cool down.	231
Boudoirs with tonka bean	6 300 g 350 g 20 g 18 g	eggs sugar flour baking powder tonka bean, ground a little more sugar	Pre-heat the oven to 170 °C. Whisk the eggs and caster sugar into a froth. Sieve the remaining ingredients and fold into the frothy mixture. Pipe into boudoir shapes and sprinkle with sugar. Bake for 10 minutes in the pre-heated oven. Let the fingers cool down before removing from the mould.	230

Egg

DESCRIPTION	HOW TO PREPARE	PG
Smoked egg yolk	Place the egg yolk on a spoon and lay in a deep tray. Heat a second spoon until it is red-hot, add to the tray but not too close to the egg yolk to prevent it from cooking. Sprinkle a spoonful of ashes (gained from smoking food) onto the hot spoon and cover the tray completely with cling film so the smoke cannot escape. Leave to smoke for five minutes. Season the yolk with pepper and salt.	115

Juices

DESCRIPTION	AMOUNT	INGREDIENTS	HOW TO PREPARE	PG
Ice Tea Fruits	1 liter 60 g 125 g 375 ml 80 ml	water dried rose hips freeze-dried raspberry raspberry juice orange juice ice cubes and fresh raspberries to garnish	Bring the water to the boil and add the rose hips. Cover the casserole and simmer for 10 minutes. Turn off the heat and stir the freeze-dried raspberry into the liquid. Steep for another 10 minutes. Sieve the liquid and push all of the taste and liquid of the solids out of the sieve. Add the juices to the liquid and cool down completely. Serve with a few ice cubes and garnish with fresh raspberries.	

DESCRIPTION	AMOUNT	INGREDIENTS	HOW TO PREPARE	PG
Lapsang Souchong	2 200 ml 50 ml 50 ml 700 ml	tea spoons dried lapsang souchong sugar water whisky lemon juice water Ice cubes and lemon peel to garnish	Infuse all of the ingredients, except the garnish, in a casserole for 2 hours. Use a cheese cloth to sieve and produce a clear tea. Serve with ice cubes and lemon peel.	
Soleil vert	2 200 ml 50 ml 100 ml 3 drops 600 ml	tea spoons soleil vert tea sugar water lemon juice grapefruit juice drops of orange bitters water Ice cubes and grapefruit to garnish	Prepare an infusion of all of the ingredients and steep for 2 hours. Sieve through a cheese cloth for a clear tea. Serve on ice cubes and garnish with a slice of grapefruit.	158

Vegetables

DESCRIPTION	AMOUNT	INGREDIENTS	HOW TO PREPARE	PG
Potato puffs		oil for frying 1 potato corn starch egg white	Heat the deep fryer up to 180 °C. Cut one potato into slices with a thickness of 0.5mm. Transfer to a chopping board and pat dry. Spread a very thin layer of egg white onto a potato slice. Coat another slice with corn starch, using a sieve. Blow away the excess corn starch and press the two slices together, using a bit of force. Then, make circle shapes in the desired size and slip into the hot frying oil. Using a spoon, cover the top of the circle with hot oil so both sides are cooked at the same time. When the disc is golden brown and has a lovely puffiness, carefully remove from the frying oil and drain. Add a little bit of salt to taste.	111
Beetroot cooked in hay; BLOODY BEETY		salt white pepper freshly grated horseradish cabernet sauvignon vinegar leaves of red shiso, finely chopped	Pre-heat the oven to 170 °C. Cover the bottom of an oven-proof casserole in hay. Place whole beetroot on top. Make sure that you don't cram the casserole full of beetroot and that you don't stack the vegetables. Arrange a layer of hay on top of the beetroot and cover with a lid. Slow-cook in the pre-heated oven until the beets are completely cooked (if you can make a dent with your finger, they are ready). Cool down in the hay. Peel the beetroot and dehydrate for approx. 3 hours at 80 °C. Pass through the mincer and season.	

Onion finger food — 105

AMOUNT	INGREDIENTS
1,5 kg	onions
	butter
	thyme
200 ml	chicken stock
10 g	liquorice paste
1 g	Xanthan gum
0,5 g	white pepper, ground
8	gelatine leaves
2 g	agar agar
50 g	dried hibiscus
5 g	sansho pepper
	A leaf of red-veined dock to garnish

Pre-heat the oven to 180 °C.
Deprive the onions of their bottoms and fry the de-bottomed side in butter, in a hot casserole, until almost black. Be careful! The onions have to be roasted but not burnt to a crisp. Put the lid back onto the casserole and cook in the oven for around 15 minutes at 180 °C or until the onions are cooked through.
Push out the inner four layers and set aside; the skins will be used as a covering.
Fry the remaining onion, without its skin, in oil adding a little thyme. Cover and cook in the oven at 160 °C for 45 minutes.
Mix one kilogram of the cooked onion with the chicken stock, the liquorice paste, the Xanthan gum, the white pepper, the gelatine and the agar agar.
Mix into a fine cream and pipe into silicon mats (preferably, small quenelle shapes, this cream will provide the filling for the inner onion segments).
Allow the cream to set in the fridge before placing it in the freezer. This will make it so much easier to remove from the mould.
Mix the dried hibiscus with the sansho pepper into a fine powder and sprinkle over the dessert.
Garnish with a leaf of red-veined dock.

CABBAGE

Cabbage dish
Cabbage croquant — 94-6

Bring water to the boil and add salt to taste. Blanch the cabbage leaves briefly and cool down in iced water.
Dry out on a piece of cloth. Heat the oil in the deep fryer up to 180 °C.
Deep-fry the cabbage leaves until all the liquid has evaporated. Pat dry and sprinkle with salt.

Cabbage chutney with redcurrant
For the roast garlic:

AMOUNT	INGREDIENTS
200 g	kale, grilled
50 g	spring onion, grilled
50 g	lemon oil
60 g	redcurrants, roast
2 g	salt
20 g	roast garlic
15 ml	lemon juice

Roast entire bulbs of garlic in a 180°C for 12 minutes.
Then push the cloves out of their skins.
Finely chop the kale. Slice the spring onions vertically and then chop finely into half rings.
Pour the lemon oil into a hot frying pan and briefly heat the cabbage and spring onion.
Add the roast redcurrants and the salt.
Grind the roast garlic into a paste and mix with the cabbage and onions.
Add the lemon juice and cool down.

AUBERGINE

Steamed aubergine

AMOUNT	INGREDIENTS
550 g	aubergine, peeled but left entire
55 g	brown ponzu
0,3 g	jasmine tea
5,5 g	salt

Vacuum all of the ingredients and steam at 94 °C until cooked – this will take approx. 40 minutes.
Remove from the bag and cut each aubergine into three slices.
Fry on both sides in a little oil until a lovely golden brown.
Add salt to taste.

DESCRIPTION	AMOUNT	INGREDIENTS	HOW TO PREPARE	PG
Pickled baby aubergine	200 g	sake	Bring the liquids to the boil and cool down completely. Vacuum the baby aubergines with the pickling liquid and ferment for at least 1 week.	
	150 g	sushi vinegar		
	100 g	mirin		
	50 g	dashi vinegar		
	6	baby aubergines		
Dehydrated aubergine	100 g	coffee oil (500 g oil, 7 g ground coffee, vacuum and warm sous-vide for 3 hours at 85 °C. Sieve through a cloth)	For the coffee vinaigrette, blend all of the ingredients apart from the aubergines. Roast the aubergines above a hot flame and peel. Vacuum with the coffee vinaigrette. Cook at 94 °C for around 30 minutes Cut into slices and dehydrate for approx. 2 hours at 80 °C.	
	20 g	lemon oil		
	30 g	lemon juice		
	10 g	sushi vinegar		
	10 g	mirin		
	10 g	ginger syrup		
	3 g	salt		
	0,1 g	cinnamon		
	0,3 g	ground white pepper		
	4	aubergines		
Tartare of aubergine	2	aubergines	Cut the aubergines in half, brush with olive oil, and sprinkle over some salt. Cook in a 180 °C oven for 30 minutes. Scoop the flesh form the aubergine and chop finely. Blend 350 grams of aubergine flesh with the other ingredients. Season with salt and/or pepper if you like.	
	3,5 g	salt		
	0,3 g	white pepper		
	10 g	sushi vinegar		
	0,2 g	cinnamon powder		
	0,2 g	cumin powder		
	0,1 g	cayenne pepper		

TOMATO

DESCRIPTION	AMOUNT	INGREDIENTS	HOW TO PREPARE	PG
Tomato chutney	20 g	shallot, finely diced	Fry the shallots in a little oil. Add the sugar and caramelise. Add the tomatoes. Briefly turn up the heat, stirring all the time. Add the remaining ingredients and reduce on low heat until most of the liquid has evaporated. Finally, season with a dash of lemon juice and salt to taste.	
	20 g	sugar		
	200 g	brunoise of tomatoes, peeled and de-seeded		
	20 g	dry sherry		
	20 g	sherry vinegar		
	20 g	lemon juice		
	2 g	coriander seed, toasted		
	2 g	cumin, ground		
		zest of 1 lemon		
	2 dashes	of red tabasco		
		salt to taste (only after the chutney is cooked)		

'Leaky' tomatoes

Amount	Ingredients
2,5 kg	tomatoes
20 g	garlic
25 g	lemon verbena
25 g	lemon thyme
	zest of 2 lemons
25 g	thyme
10 g	salt
4	black peppercorns
25 g	white wine vinegar
Add to taste:	salt
	freshly squeezed lemon juice
	ginger juice
	red Tabasco
	white wine vinegar

This is where your blender comes into its own. Pour in the tomatoes together with the garlic, lemon verbena, lemon thyme, lemon zest, ordinary thyme, salt, black pepper and white wine vinegar. Chop the ingredients roughly: you should be able to identify every single herb and vegetable used in the preparation of this recipe. If you grind your ingredients to a pulp, you can't extract the juices.
Now transfer the tomato mixture into a cheese cloth and drain above a bowl. In a cold environment like a cellar, this is likely to take 24 hours.
Retrieve the 'leaky juices' and season with the other ingredients.

Yellow cherry tomatoes

Peel the tomatoes and flavour with salt, white pepper and ginger juice. De-hydrate the tomatoes for 3-4 hours at 70 °C.

Green tiger tomatoes

Amount	Ingredients
500 g	base oil
150 g	lemon thyme
4 g	salt
10	green tiger tomatoes
To taste or as required:	salt
	white pepper
	lemon thyme oil to taste

To prepare the lemon thyme oil, vacuum the base - or neutral - oil together with the lemon thyme and the salt. Slow-cook at 85 °C for 3 hours.
Pass through a cloth and then through a sieve.
Quarter the tomatoes and then again to end up with eight parts.
Season with salt, white pepper and lemon thyme oil.
Now dehydrate the tomato parts, for 2 to 3 hours, at 70 °C.

Tomato chutney

Amount	Ingredients
1 kg	tomatoes
700 g	sugar
200 g	sliced lemon, de-seeded but skin left on
80 g	apple vinegar
20 g	tikka masala spices

Add everything to a large casserole and simmer away until the mixture is reduced by 75%. Remove from the hob and cool down.

LETTUCE

Emulsion of lettuce

	Amount	Ingredients
A:	60 g	egg-white
	2 g	xanthan gum
	40 g	chardonnay vinegar
	10 g	lemon juice
	10 g	lime juice
	10 g	jalapeñosap
	15 g	ginger juice
	15 g	ginger sirop
	300 g	puree of lettuce (see description)
B:	50 g	linseed oil
	300 g	grape seed oil
	7 g	salt

For the lettuce puree: blanch 400 grams of lettuce and 100 grams of spinach. Scare in ice water and mix everything into puree in a blender.
Place everything from group A in a measuring cup and mix with a hand blender for 3 minutes until smooth.
Then slowly add the oil from group B while you continue to mix.
Finish with the salt.
Keep cold.

DESCRIPTION	AMOUNT	INGREDIENTS	HOW TO PREPARE	PG
Gravy of lettuce	150 g	lettuce juice	Mix everything in a measuring cup with a hand blender to a smooth gravy and pass through a fine sieve.	
	30 g	celery juice	(Note: the gravy starts to discolour after about 5 hours.)	
	25 g	spinach juice		
	10 g	ginger juice		
	15 g	ginger sirop		
	4 g	jalapeño juice		
	10 g	lemon juice		
	3 g	salt		
	0,5 g	xanthan gum		
Chutney, lettuce and buckwheat	175 g	parboiled and squeezed lettuce	Cut the lettuce into small pieces.	
		ginger marmelade	Chop the pickled jalapeño and ginger marmalade through the lettuce.	
	35 g	pickled jalapeño	Add all remaining ingredients and mix until well blended.	
	15 g	juice of pickled jalapeño	Season with salt if necessary.	
	5 g	chardonnay vinegar	(Note: this chutney discolours after about 5 hours.)	
	5 g	buckwheat, boiled		
	120 g	linseed oil		
	15 g	dark soy sauce		
	2 g			
Sucrine pickled in Savora mustard vinaigrette	30 g	Savora mustard	Mix everything in a measuring cup using a whisk.	
	10 g	dashi vinegar	Cut the sucrine into 4 parts and draw vacuum with the savora vinaigrette.	
	10 g	yellow ponzu	Let marinate for 1 hour.	
	10 g	sushi vinegar	You can use mustard flowers or mizuna lettuce as a garnish.	
	10 g	water		
	20 g	lemon juice		
	100 ml	grape seed oil		
	1	sucrine		
Interpretations of risotto	We all know risotto as a dish with rice, but we enjoy experimenting with other products to create different structures and flavours. For example, we have a risotto with four different grains, one with buckwheat, one with celeriac, and so on. There is endless variation with different types of risotto. Scooping cooked cereals through a vegetable cream is the easiest way to experiment! There are endless combinations and you can go anywhere. You should also try to vary with crunch and texture. If you put that through your risotto at the last minute, you create yet another layer.			137

DESCRIPTION	AMOUNT	INGREDIENTS	HOW TO PREPARE	PG
Violet potatoes cooked in hay and clay (straight from the pits)	1 kg	violet potatoes	Fill a large pot with water and hay. Season slightly with salt. Bring to the boil and add the potatoes. Let it simmer gently until the potatoes are fully cooked. Drain and leave the potatoes cooling down. Cut the potatoes in half and make a hole in the middle with a spoon. Save the 'waste'. Mix the clay powder little by little with water until you get a porridge with the consistency of yogurt. Paste the clay mixture onto the potato and put in an oven at 50 ° C until the clay layer is hard. Mix the ingredients for the filling with a hand blender and carefully add a neutral oil (e.g. sunflower oil) until you get a nice thickness. Fill the cavity in the potato with the herb mayonnaise and the other ingredients.	53
	100 g	clay powder		
		hay		
		water		
		salt		
For the filling:	100 g	chopped potato 'waste'		
	20 g	capers, chopped		
	20 g	shallot, finely chopped		
	5 g	chives, finely chopped		
	4 g	salt		
	80 g	herb mayonnaise		
For the herb mayonnaise:	80 g	egg yolk		
	20 ml	lemon juice		
	20 ml	vinegar		
	10 g	fine mustard		
	2 g	salt		
	20 g	persil, chopped		
	10 g	sage, chopped		
	2 g	garlic, chopped		
Poached fish in smoked milk			Salt the fish in the usual way: 8 grams of salt for 1 kilogram of fish. Put a bowl of milk in a larger stainless steel container and heat a spoon hot red. Place the spoon in the large container next to the bowl. Drop a spoonful of wood chips for smoking on the hot spoon and cover the container well with plastic wrap so that no smoke can escape. Let rest until the smoke has cleared up. Heat the milk to around 60 ° C. Poach the fish. Ensure that the milk remains at 60 ° C throughout the entire process.	86-7
Hop shoots			We cook our hop shoots in a blanc (water with flour, salt and lemon juice). By adding another beer (in this case an IPA) we re-emphasize the hop shoots, because beer also has that hoppy and bitter touch. The freshness in the beer makes it complete. We have added radish and pomegranate to the dish to add a sour touch. Hop shoots are in themselves a fantastic product and therefore do not need much.	88-9

Description	Amount	Ingredients	How to prepare	PG
Buttermilk with dill oil	300 g	dill	Mix the ingredients for the oil in a blender for 12 minutes, at the highest speed. Sieve through a cloth so that only the oil remains.	118-9
For the dill oil:	1000 ml	neutral oil	Finely chop the vegetables and sauté them with the salt and oil. Deglaze with the Noilly Prat and the chicken broth.	
	6 g	salt	Add the cream and simmer for 1 hour.	
For the juice of buttermilk:	40 g	shallot	Mix everything in a blender to a smooth sauce and add 100 g of cold butter cubes. Pass through a fine sieve.	
	65 g	celery	Season with buttermilk, lemon juice and a pinch of salt (to taste).	
	150 g	green apple	Heat the whole thing again before use and create a small foam layer with a hand blender.	
	40 g	white mushrooms	Finish with a few drops of dill oil.	
	15 g	salt		
	30 g	oil		
	50 g	Noilly Prat		
	1000 ml	chicken stock		
	200 g	cream		
	100 g	butter		
	175 g	buttermilk		
	40 g	lemon juice		
		salt		

Description	Amount	Ingredients	How to prepare	PG
Pickled radish and seaweed roll	200 g	saké	Mix all the ingredients for the pickle base and set aside.	90
For the pickle base	150 g	sushi vinegar	Cut the daikon into strips of 0.5 x 0.5 cm and a length of 10 cm.	
	100 g	mirin	Place the daikon bars in the pickle base and let it pickle for at least 1 week (preferably vacuum drawn or in a sealed container).	
	50 g	dashi vinegar	Remove the daikon strips from the bath and gently pat them dry.	
	1 stuk	daikon	Make a roll: wrap each strip individually with a piece of nori and then wrap them in 10 bigger strips of nori.	
			Roll in plastic wrap and lay in the fridge to rest. The nori needs time to rehydrate itself.	
			Cut slices of 1 cm thick with a sharp knife and remove the foil.	

RECIPES WITH WHITE ASPARAGUS FROM WERCHTER

Description	Amount	Ingredients	How to prepare	PG
Asparagus salad	10	asparagus	Peel and grate the asparagus with a grater.	
For the infusion of lemon melissa		salt	Add salt to taste and drain on a sieve for 2 hours to remove excess moisture.	
	100 g	lemon melissa	Vacuum the ingredients for the infusion and heat for 3 hours at 70 ° C.	
	500 ml	grape seed oil	Allow to cool and sieve through a cloth.	
For the vinaigrette	1	lemon peel	In a measuring cup, mix all the ingredients for the vinaigrette with a whisk.	
	25 g	mint	Season the asparagus with the vinaigrette of lemon melissa.	
	3 g	salt		
	300 g	lemon melissa		
	50 g	lemon juice, sieved		
	50 g	sushi vinegar		
	4 g	salt		
	10 g	ginger vinegar		

DESCRIPTION	AMOUNT	INGREDIENTS	HOW TO PREPARE	PG
Cooked white asparagus tips			Vacuum 200 grams of asparagus tips with 2 grams of salt and 10 grams of lemon melissa oil (see previous recipe). Cook for 12 minutes at 85 ° C. Cool in ice water.	
Spaghetti of asparagus			Cut thin asparagus julienne, about 10 centimeters in length. Briefly blanch in salted water and cool in ice water. Heat some butter in a pan and add the asparagus. Season with grated nutmeg, lemon juice, white pepper and some salt. Turn with a meat fork to form a nice roll.	
Classically cooked white asparagus	5 litres 2 kg 300 g	water peeled asparagus dairy butter salt	Place the asparagus in cold water and add the butter. Add salt to taste. Place some baking paper on top so that the asparagus stays under water. This avoids uneven cooking. Bring the water to the boil and cook for 1 minute. Remove and place the pan with the asparagus in the fridge. Allow to cool completely. Heat the desired amount in the cooking water. Remove the asparagus from the cooking liquid as soon as they are hot and finish with grated nutmeg, white pepper, salt and lemon zest.	
Lightly smoked white asparagus			Place the cooked asparagus in a stainless steel container, which in turn goes into a larger stainless steel container. Heat a spoon until it is red hot and place it in the large container. Place the spoon in the large container next to the bowl. Drop a spoonful of wood chips for smoking on the hot spoon and cover the container well with plastic wrap so that no smoke can escape. Let the smoke rest for 10 minutes. Heat the asparagus in a little cooking liquid and season with salt or pepper if necessary.	
Fried white asparagus			Cut some cooked asparagus tops in half. Heat a dash of oil in a frying pan. Place the asparagus in the pan, with the flat side down. Colour until they look golden brown. Add a knob of butter and a little cooking liquid from the asparagus. Shake the pan occasionally until almost all of the moisture has evaporated. This way you get a nice layer of butter around the asparagus. Remove from the pan. Season with white pepper and any salt to taste.	91

Colophon

www.lannoo.com

Register on our web site and we will regularly send you a newsletter with information about new books and interesting, exclusive offers.

TEXT: Bart De Pooter en Robby Sallaets
PHOTOGRAPHY: Kris Vlegels
GRAPHIC DESIGN: Grietje Uytdenhouwen (Papil)

CREDITS: p 10 *(David Legreve)* | p 35, 36-37, 38-39, 50, 52, 56 *(Bart Van Leuven)* | p 63 *(Adriaan Van Looy)* | p 82-83 *(Electrolux)* p 184 *(Helge Kirchberger Photography / Red Bull Hangar-7)*

If you have observations or questions, please contact our editorial office: redactielifestyle@lannoo.com

D/2019/45/423 – NUR 440
ISBN 978 94 014 6265 5